DATE DUE			

B
VILLA

13FL00656

Marcovitz, Hal.

Pancho Villa

**GAVIT MIDDLE/HIGH SCHOOL
HAMMOND, INDIANA**

780122 02295   31832C   002

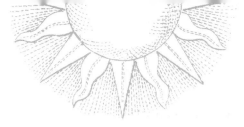

THE GREAT
HISPANIC HERITAGE

Pancho Villa

THE GREAT HISPANIC HERITAGE

THE GREAT
HISPANIC HERITAGE

Pancho Villa

Hal Marcovitz

CHELSEA HOUSE
PUBLISHERS
A Haights Cross Communications Company

Philadelphia

CHELSEA HOUSE PUBLISHERS
VP, NEW PRODUCT DEVELOPMENT Sally Cheney
DIRECTOR OF PRODUCTION Kim Shinners
CREATIVE MANAGER Takeshi Takahashi
MANUFACTURING MANAGER Diann Grasse

Staff for PANCHO VILLA
ASSISTANT EDITOR Kate Sullivan
PRODUCTION EDITOR Jaimie Winkler
PHOTO EDITOR Sarah Bloom
SERIES & COVER DESIGNER Terry Mallon
LAYOUT 21st Century Publishing and Communications, Inc.

A Haights Cross Communications ➤ Company

http://www.chelseahouse.com

First Printing

1 3 5 7 9 8 6 4 2

Library of Congress Cataloging-in-Publication Data

Marcovitz, Hal.
   Pancho Villa / Hal Marcovitz.
       p. cm.— (The great Hispanic heritage)
Includes index.
   ISBN 0-7910-7257-6
   1. Villa, Pancho, 1878-1923—Juvenile literature. 2. Mexico—History—
1910–1946—Juvenile literature. I. Title. II. Series.
F1234.V63 M37 2002
972.08'1'092—dc21

                                                    2002015203

Table of Contents

1

Escape from Santiago Tlatelolco

Mexico City was alive with the sights, sounds and smells of a vibrant capital undergoing dynamic change. In the crowded public square, known as the *zócalo*, vendors sold fruits, blankets and serapes to customers. To quiet their children, parents may have spent a few coins to buy them honey cakes, tortillas and *horchata*, a soft drink made of fruit juice and almonds. While mothers shopped and kept an eye on the young ones, fathers had the opportunity to visit Mexico City's public drinking houses, known as the *pulquerías*.

It is likely that during the fall and winter of 1912, talk in the *pulquerías* centered on the revolution that had been raging for two years. Mexico had always been a country where civil turmoil was a part of everyday life, but the last two years had been a particularly violent period in the country's history. Mexicans had seen the dynasty of long-time dictator Porfirio Díaz crumble under the weight of scandal and abuse of power. Poor and illiterate peasants,

6

Mexican rebel Pancho Villa astride his horse. Villa, known in the United States as the "Mexican Robin Hood," fought to improve the lives of Mexican peasants.

caught up in the fervor of the revolution, flocked to join the ranks of swaggering leaders.

One of those leaders was Pancho Villa, a robust,

raw-boned and jovial man who had risen from common bandit to head a powerful peasant army composed of thousands of volunteers, most of them from the northern Mexican state of Chihuahua. They were drawn to Villa by his bravery, and by his daring and skillful horsemanship. But also, unlike many of the men with power and influence in Mexico, they regarded Villa as a man of the people, sincere in his desire to improve the lives of the *peóns* who labored in the fields of the *haciendas* while the rich land barons, many of them from America, grew wealthier and wealthier. Indeed, in Chihuahua Villa was known as the "Friend of the Poor." Newspapers in the United States labeled Villa the "Mexican Robin Hood."

But in late 1912, the popular rebel leader found himself imprisoned in Mexico City. Villa had been arrested in Chihuahua on the orders of General Victoriano Huerta, his crafty and hard-hearted military superior, who believed he had to get rid of Villa before he could make his own bid for power. Huerta charged Villa with theft and insubordination—he accused Villa of stealing two horses as well as encouraging his men to disregard orders. Huerta ordered Villa to face a firing squad, but the 11th-hour intervention of President Francisco Madero saved the rebel's life.

During the first two years of the revolution Villa had been immensely helpful to Madero, leading battles against opponents who sought to topple the president in order to take power for themselves. Just a few months before Huerta ordered Villa's arrest, Villa led the defense of the Chihuahuan town of Parral, which had been in danger of falling to Pascual Orozco Jr., a Madero opponent who had the backing of wealthy citizens of Chihuahua. They worried that a peasant uprising would cost them their lands, fortunes and, quite possibly, their lives.

While in prison, Villa wrote many letters to Madero asking for clemency.

"I am one of your friends who wishes you happiness," Villa wrote to Madero in July 1912. He continued:

> Though I do not know how many bad things they may have told you about me, I swear to you that I shall be loyal . . . You will never hear signs of adulation from me, since I am a man of firm convictions who knows how to suffer. I suffer from the depth of my heart, but I am not complaining to you about my suffering, since man was created to suffer.

Villa may have constantly tried to prove his loyalty to Madero, but the president had no mind to order Villa's release. Madero didn't trust Villa. Nor did U.S. Ambassador Henry Lane Wilson.

VICTORIANO HUERTA

In a country plagued by deceitful, ambitious and greedy leaders, Victoriano Huerta stands out as perhaps the most notorious scoundrel in the history of Mexico. He was a wily and merciless army general, an alcoholic and possibly a drug addict. His scheming ways enabled him to seize power in Mexico, but he was unable to maintain his hold over the national government for long.

He was born in 1845, a member of the Huichol tribe of Indians from the Mexican state of Jalisco. He learned to read and write as a young boy, a rare accomplishment for a poor Indian. Huerta entered Military College and was awarded a commission in the army. Huerta was an influential general during the latter years of the administration of President Porfirio Díaz. He survived the downfall of Díaz, but betrayed the democratically elected Francisco Madero, ordering the president's assassination and seizing power in February 1913. He headed the government for just over a year, ruling through the use of terror and murder. Finally, rebel forces overran his troops and he was forced to flee. Huerta died while under arrest in a U.S. Army stockade near El Paso, Texas, in 1916.

America's envoy to Mexico regarded Villa as an uncouth and uneducated bandit. Wilson pressed Madero to keep Villa in jail. Unknown to the president, Wilson was secretly helping Huerta make plans to oust Madero and assume the leadership of the government.

Ambassador Wilson pressured Madero to bring Villa to trial. Finally, Madero relented and ordered Villa transferred to Mexico City. By December 1912, Villa had spent some seven months in prison while military prosecutors prepared a case against the rebel leader based on Huerta's bogus charges.

Meanwhile, the fervor of the revolution continued to burn in Mexico, and particularly in Chihuahua. The governor of Chihuahua, Abraham González, was an ally of Villa and had asked Madero to release his friend, but Madero refused. Militias composed of Chihuahua peasants were loyal to González and Villa, and were able to hold off Pascual Orozco and his followers. But their efforts were constantly undermined by federal troops, who took their orders from Huerta. The federal soldiers often harassed the peasant militia fighters while Madero refused to send González money from the federal treasury to pay the militia volunteers. While all this was happening in Chihuahua, Villa could do nothing but sit in his jail cell.

"I have been loyal to you and I shall remain so since I am not swayed by money," Villa insisted in a letter to the president, in one of several appeals to Madero for clemency.

His letter concluded: "I ask you for justice; I am tired of doing so and if you cannot grant it to me, I ask you in the name of justice to have a meeting of ministers so that it can be established who was right. One of the reasons for my bad luck is that I am a man without culture and I do not know how to defend my right. I ask for justice and I say good-bye to you with love and respect as always. Farewell, Sir."

Alas, the revolutionary leader would get no justice from Francisco Madero. The president refused to answer Villa's letters. What's more, the case against Villa proceeded toward

Francisco Madero served as president of Mexico from 1911 to 1913. Although Villa repeatedly pledged his support for Madero while in prison, Madero refused to release Villa.

trial. In September 1912, the court refused a motion by Villa's attorneys to dismiss the charges. It had finally become apparent to Pancho Villa that he would have to stand trial on the wily Huerta's trumped-up accusations, and it was likely the court would be in Huerta's pocket.

And so Villa made plans to escape.

Villa was not without resources. Friends on the outside provided money for him, which he used to bribe the guards for favors. Inside the jail, Villa was immensely popular among the other prisoners because he often used his money to buy favors for them as well. What's more, though, he was a natural leader whose charisma ignited the patriotism of his fellow prisoners, who hoped to join the revolutionary cause after their releases. Indeed, many of the other prisoners had been sent to jail because they found themselves on the wrong side of the revolution, and Huerta aimed to keep them out of his way.

Villa's first attempt to break out of prison failed. By making bribes to the guards, Villa obtained a set of keys for his cell as well as the cell of Gildardo Magaña, a friend and follower of Emiliano Zapata, a rebel leader from southern Mexico. Villa paid bribes to the guards to look the other way as the two men left the jail, but after letting themselves out of their cells and taking just a few steps, they saw that guards were stationed just outside the cellblock. Villa concluded that it was a trap, and that both he and Magaña would be shot while attempting their escape. The two men quickly returned to their cells. "Only then did I realize the magnitude of the danger I faced," Magaña wrote later.

Pancho Villa believed things were now hopeless, and that he would soon be facing trial followed by a long prison term and, quite possibly, the firing squad. But events outside the Mexico City jail were unfolding in his favor, improving his chances to make a successful escape.

Félix Díaz, a nephew of the deposed Porfirio Díaz, had led his own uprising against Madero, but was captured and sent to a military prison in Mexico City known as Santiago Tlatelolco. Even though Díaz was in jail, he still had influential friends on the outside and made plans to continue his uprising. Díaz believed Pancho Villa could be drafted to help topple Madero. Díaz directed an influential lawyer, José Bonales Sandoval, to obtain Villa's transfer from the Mexico City jail to the nearby military prison.

The ploy worked. Madero, who no doubt was preoccupied with the many other plots to overthrow him, agreed to Sandoval's petition and Villa was transferred to Santiago Tlatelolco. It has never been clear why Madero agreed to the transfer, but it is

Félix Díaz led uprisings against President Madero. Díaz arranged for Villa's transfer from a Mexico City jail to a military prison in 1912, leading to Villa's eventual escape from prison.

likely the president was growing more distrustful of Huerta and believed that he would eventually need to call on Villa's loyalty. Whatever the motivation may have been for Madero's sudden change in heart, Pancho Villa was escorted into the Santiago Tlatelolco military prison in November 1912, where he immediately started making plans to escape.

The manner in which Villa escaped from Santiago Tlatelolco would seem to have been drawn right out of the pages of a western dime novel of the era. Soon after arriving in Santiago Tlatelolco, Villa made friends with Carlitos Jauregui, a young prison clerk. Certainly, Villa worked his charisma on Jauregui, who was taken with the revolutionary leader's sincerity and commitment to the poor people of Mexico. It is also likely that a few bribes may have been passed to Jauregui to gain his help in Villa's escape. Whatever his motivation, Jauregui smuggled a hacksaw, a bottle of machine oil, black wax and a suit of clothing into Villa's cell.

For three nights, Villa worked on sawing the vertical bars in his cell window, while the prison guards slept nearby. He used the machine oil to deaden the sound of the hacksaw tearing through the heavy metal bars. After each night of sawing, Villa would carefully clean up the metal shavings and cover up the saw marks on the bars with the black wax. The work was finished on Christmas Eve. The escape was planned for the next morning.

Villa rose on Christmas morning, dressed in the suit of clothes that Jauregui had smuggled in. After making the final cuts through the bars, Villa pushed them aside and wriggled out of the cell window. Jauregui waited for Villa in the prison yard. The two men then walked casually through the yard, making it appear as though they were engaged in a deep conversation. The guards nodded toward the two men and waved them through. Villa, dressed in the suit and hiding his face in a handkerchief, stirred no special interest among the guards, who may have believed he was an attorney leaving the jail after conferring with a client. After a few minutes, Villa and Jauregui walked through the gates of Santiago Tlatelolco. After seven months of imprisonment, Pancho Villa was now a free man.

Ever the showman, Villa had wanted to escape in grand style —revealing his true identity just on the other side of the wall, then mounting a horse and galloping off at the head of a group of rebels, guns blazing and shouting "Viva Villa!" as they rode through the streets of the Mexican capital. Jauregui convinced him to do otherwise. Clearly, Jauregui said, a group of armed men on horseback waiting outside the walls of Santiago Tlatelolco on Christmas morning would arouse suspicion. What's more, the clerk argued, Villa's loyal men from Chihuahua were unfamiliar with the streets of Mexico City, and might become lost in the city while making their getaway, if they were to come pick him up. So, instead of a group of rifle-toting and bandoleer-wearing rebels waiting for their leader outside the walls of Santiago Tlatelolco, Villa stepped outside the prison gates to find a car and driver arranged by Jauregui. The young prison clerk, knowing that he would eventually be discovered as Villa's confederate, had no choice but to accompany the rebel leader on his getaway.

The two men fled to the nearby city of Toluca. From Toluca, they made their way by train and ship to the United States, where they slipped into the country. Villa found refuge in the border town of El Paso, Texas, where he would plan his return to Mexico to free his people from their oppressors, once and for all.

2

"To Free Her From the Snakes"

The state of Chihuahua stretches over some 97,000 square miles in northern Mexico. It is a harsh, unforgiving territory composed mostly of rocky deserts and mountains. Few rivers flow through Chihuahua, which means little irrigation for its farmland, although some adept farmers have been able to grow crops in its dry soil. Some of the state's most fertile pasturelands are in the central part of the state and have helped support a cattle trade. After the Spanish conquered Mexico in 1521, they discovered rich silver deposits in Chihuahua. The state became a mining center for Mexico, although few natives of Chihuahua shared in the wealth. That money went into the pockets of the Spanish conquistadors. Still, native Indians found work in the silver mines, until in the mid-18th century hostile Apache Indians from the north started a series of raids on the miners, which temporarily shut down the mines, and thus terminated this source of income.

The Spaniards certainly didn't want to give up the wealth that

Chihuahua, located in the north of central Mexico, was the site of Villa's early years.

awaited them beneath the rocky Chihuahua soil. So the Spaniards offered lucrative grants of land and other rewards for migrants from Spain and central Mexico to settle in Chihuahua and help tame the wild country. To protect the settlers, the Spanish army dispatched soldiers to northern Mexico. Even

Apaches were offered food and grants of land if they agreed to settle down and stop harassing the miners. By the late 1700s, a relative calm had settled over Chihuahua.

In 1810, the first shots in the war for Mexican independence were fired when a rebellion broke out under the leadership of Miguel Hidalgo, a priest from a small central Mexican village. Soon, the Hidalgo revolution attracted some 100,000 poor Mexicans to the ranks of the rebel army. Fighting erupted all over Mexico, but in Chihuahua followers of Hidalgo found little support for the rebellion. The people of Chihuahua were mostly satisfied with the status quo and unwilling to support the rebellion. Many of them took up arms and fought on the side of the Spanish. As for Hidalgo, he was soon captured by the royalist army and executed. In fact, he was hanged in Chihuahua.

By the middle of the 19th century, life was a lot different in Chihuahua. By then, Mexicans had long since won their independence from Spain, but with just a few exceptions, their efforts at self-rule were dominated by dictators, bloody coup d'etats (sudden, violent overthrows of existing governments), intervention by foreign powers and constant upheaval. With the government in Mexico City often in a state of chaos, few officials had the inclination to pay attention to remote Chihuahua, where hostile Indian raids again became a problem. In the town of Namiquipa, residents drafted a petition asking for protection from the savage Apaches, claiming "all neighboring *haciendas* had been abandoned because of the constant danger of aggression by the barbarians between 1832 and 1860, and only Namiquipa remained to fight the barbarians and to constitute a lonely bastion of civilization in this remote region."

Their pleas fell on deaf ears. The government in Mexico City did little to protect them.

As a result, many citizens of Chihuahua fled south to the safety of Mexico City. The people who chose to remain were mostly poor. They managed to scratch out a living trying to make crops grow out of the arid soil, or as hands on cattle ranches. There is no question that the people of Chihuahua who chose to remain were a hardy, rough-and-tumble lot. After all, for years they were forced to defend themselves against the Apache raids with no help from the government in Mexico City. By the late 1800s, the Indian threat eased and the wealthy landowners— the oligarchy— returned to Chihuahua, fully expecting to re-establish their *haciendas* and dominance over society.

By the 1890s, Chihuahua was the center of what was developing into an ugly class struggle. On the one hand, the land was populated by long-time residents who had endured decades of poverty and danger from Indian attacks but had steadfastly remained in the territory. On the other hand, there was a new class of wealthy Mexicans who had spent the past 40 years sheltered in the safety of the capital, absentee landowners who were now eager to reclaim what they believed what was rightfully theirs.

That was the hostile and unsteady society in which a young boy named Doroteo Arango would grow into manhood and become the great rebel leader known as Pancho Villa.

Doroteo was born on June 5, 1878, on Rancho de la Coyotada, one of the largest *haciendas* in the state of Durango, just below Chihuahua. His parents, Agustín Arango and Micaela Arambula, were sharecroppers on the *hacienda*. They didn't own the land they farmed, and shared the profits from their crops with the *hacienda* owner, the López Negrete family.

For the first years of his life, Doroteo Arango led a normal, unremarkable life. His father died when Doroteo was young. Since he was the oldest male child in a large family, the responsibilities of the father fell on his shoulders. Like his father, Doroteo worked as a sharecropper on the López Negrete property. It is possible that he would have lived out his life sharecropping on the *hacienda*, had he not learned at the age of 16 that Don Agustín López Negrete, the *hacendado*— master of the *hacienda*—had raped his 12-year-old sister, Martina.

Although the accounts of this story vary—over the years, Pancho Villa also blamed others for the rape—there is no question that Doroteo believed that as head of the Arango family it became his responsibility to avenge the crime. Doroteo found a gun at the house of a cousin, tracked down Don Agustín and shot him.

The shot hit Don Agustín in the foot. When five of the *hacienda* owner's men arrived to see what the commotion was about, they drew their guns and prepared to shoot the boy who had wounded their boss. But Doroteo's life was spared by Don Agustín, who commanded them to put down their guns. "Don't kill this boy," he said. "Take me home."

Although he knew that, at least for now, Don Agustín had spared his life, Doroteo feared arrest and imprisonment. So he found a horse and fled into the mountains of Durango and later Chihuahua.

"My conscience told me I had done the right thing," Villa later wrote. "The master, with five armed men, with all the power at his disposal, had tried to impose a forced contribution of our honor. The sweat of his serfs, the work of his serfs, our constant and tiring labor in order to enrich him, the master, was not sufficient for him. He also needed our women. His despotism led to the profanation of our home."

From that day on, Doroteo Arango led the life of an outlaw—a *bandido.* Cattle rustling was his specialty, but Arango would also commit robberies. He particularly enjoyed stealing money from wealthy *hacendados* he caught alone on the trail.

During his years as a bandit, there were many close calls and narrow escapes. He was captured several times, but had an uncanny ability to slip away from officers of the law. He was an excellent horseman and daring adventurer, unafraid to shoot it out with his pursuers.

While making his way as a bandit Doroteo Arango decided to change his name. For his last name, Doroteo began calling himself Villa because his father had been the illegitimate son of a man named Jesús Villa. As a first name, he went by Francisco.

Indeed, Francisco Villa had been a familiar name in Durango for a long time. In years gone by, a man named Francisco Villa had been a notorious bandit. Perhaps, Doroteo felt inspired to model his life on the exploits of another man who lived as a *bandido.*

The mountains of Durango and Chihuahua provided a hiding place for the young Villa. Villa's life as an outlaw began at age 16, when he fled to these mountains after avenging his younger sister's rape.

He joined two other outlaws to form a gang. His cohorts were Ignacio Parra and Refugio Alvarado. The two older bandits let Villa join their gang, warning him, "Look, young man, if you want to go with us, you have to do everything that we tell you. We know how to kill and rob. We tell you this so that you should be afraid."

Soon, the new gang would prosper as the young Francisco Villa led the way with his bravura and brains. As a sharecropper on the López Negrete *hacienda*, Doroteo Arango barely had enough to eat. As a feared bandit, in just a short time Francisco

Villa amassed what was by Chihuahua standards a small fortune. Soon, Villa found himself carrying 3,000 pesos (the basic monetary unit of Mexico) in his pocket—ten times the annual wage for a Chihuahua farmer. But that was only the beginning. Villa, Parra and Alvarado robbed a wealthy mine owner and made off with 150,000 pesos. Villa's share came to 50,000 pesos. Barely 20 years old, Francisco Villa was suddenly a very wealthy man.

While Villa and his gang were rustling cattle and swooping down on wealthy *hacendados*, changes were taking place in Mexico City that would have a profound effect on the lives of everyone in Mexico.

Following the departure of the Spanish in 1821, a period of tumult dominated the Mexican government that would last until 1833, when Mexican army leader Antonio López de Santa Anna was elected president. Santa Anna's attention was immediately drawn to Texas, which at the time was under Mexican rule. Texans had been agitating for years for independence, which they hoped would eventually lead to statehood in America. In late 1835 the first shots were fired in the Texas War of Independence. Santa Anna led an army of some 5,000 soldiers into Texas to put down the rebellion. He scored a victory, albeit a costly one, when he massacred 136 Texan defenders at the Battle of the Alamo. A few weeks later, Sam Houston and his army, bent on avenging the slaughter at the Alamo, finally captured Santa Anna and defeated his troops.

Texas was declared independent and would eventually join the American union. The desire of Americans to add California and New Mexico to the United States led to the Mexican–American War in 1846. The Mexican army was defeated in the war, and Mexicans were forced to accept bitter terms.

With the federal treasury bankrupt, taxes high and the government once again in turmoil, Santa Anna made his way back to the Mexican capital and declared himself dictator. He wouldn't last long. Civil war soon broke out. A group of liberal reformers led by Benito Juárez wrested power from Santa Anna, who was exiled.

Juárez assumed the presidency in 1855. Committed to democracy, Juárez instituted a number of reforms and freedoms previously unknown in Mexico. All males were given the right to vote. Freedom of speech and other civil liberties were ensured. A constitution was written. The United States supported Juárez, but elsewhere foreign powers had devious plans for Mexico. In 1858, civil war again broke out. Juárez's opponents, many of them wealthy landowners worried about the president's ideas about distributing land to the poor peasants, initiated a bloody rebellion against the democratic government. The conservatives, who were aided by Spain, fought the Juárez government in what became known as the War of Reform. Juárez successfully fought them off, but the days of rebellion in Mexico were far from over. Juárez had always been suspicious of the Catholic Church's influence on the peasantry. In 1861, he issued decrees nation-alizing church property. Next, he declared that Mexico would no longer make interest payments on foreign loans borrowed by previous governments.

Once again, war dominated the Mexican countryside. This time, the conservatives were backed by France as well as Spain and Great Britain, which feared the loss of millions of dollars because of Mexico's refusal to honor its loans. In 1863, Juárez was ousted from the presidency. By then, Spain and Great Britain had backed away from the rebellion, leaving France to pull the puppet strings in Mexico. French leader Napoleon III installed Maximilian, the archduke of Austria, as emperor of Mexico.

Maximilian ruled for two years, but soon found that he could not rely on Napoleon to keep him in power, as demonstrated by Napoleon's withdrawal of French troops from Mexico. The United States made it clear to Napoleon that it did not favor the dictatorship of Maximilian, preferring instead that a democracy be installed just beneath its southern border. Maximilan was booted out of power and executed in 1866. He was replaced by Juárez, who remained in office until his death in 1872.

The next significant figure to arrive on the scene was Porfirio Díaz, a former theology student and lawyer who rose

Porfirio Díaz devoted himself to the military and, after ascending the army ranks, became president of Mexico in 1877. Díaz managed to remain in office for 34 years by favoring the wealthy and controlling opposition.

to the rank of general in the Mexican army. He had been a supporter of Benito Juárez, but after taking office as president in 1877 he quickly abandoned Juárez's ideas about democracy and civil rights, and assumed the role of dictator. Unlike Santa

Anna and others who chose to rule as dictators before him, Díaz proved very resilient, holding onto power for 34 years. In Mexico, the years of Díaz's rule are known as the "Porfiriato."

Díaz cracked down on dissent and made sure the rich landowners and businessmen were well-served. During Mexico's turbulent history, others before him had tried to rule in that fashion but had failed. Díaz managed to hold onto power for as long as he did by using some of his country's resources to improve the life of Mexico's poor. By stabilizing the government, foreign investors returned to Mexico, which helped create jobs. Díaz built some 8,000 miles of railroads, which meant that the crops from Mexico's farms and goods from the country's factories could now find their way to the port cities for export to Europe.

Nevertheless, life for most of Mexico's poor, hungry and landless citizens remained harsh. During Díaz's reign, medical care for Indians and *mestizos*—people of half-Indian and half-European blood—was virtually unheard of. The life expectancy for a Mexican was half the life expectancy for a European. Half the babies in Mexico died before they were a year old. In Mexico, corn was the basic food for most of the people, yet the per capita production of corn in 1910 was half what it was in 1810.

And there was no question that the people who benefited most under Porfirio Díaz were the wealthy and privileged few. They ate food and drank wine imported from Europe. They furnished the grand homes on their *haciendas* with tables and chairs carved by Europe's finest craftsmen. In 1907, when American Secretary of State Elihu Root visited Mexico City, he was given a carefully guided tour of only the finest Mexican homes. So impressed with President Díaz and what he saw of the Mexican capital, Root remarked: "If I were a Mexican, I should feel that the steadfast loyalty of a lifetime would not be too much to give in return for the blessings that he has brought to the country."

Díaz not only fooled Elihu Root, he also succeeded in fooling himself. In 1908, Díaz granted an interview to James Creelman, a journalist for *Pearson's Magazine.* So sure of his popularity and believing that the course he had set for the Mexican people was the proper one, the 78-year-old Díaz boasted that Mexico was now ready for democracy and he would permit free elections in 1910. In fact, Díaz told Creelman, he had no interest in running for the office himself and was sure a new leader would emerge from among the Mexican people. Of course, what Díaz really had in mind was that his hand-chosen successor would emerge from among the Mexican people, and that Díaz would serve as the true power behind the presidency.

One Mexican who read the *Pearson's Magazine* interview with interest was Francisco Madero. Like Díaz, Madero also believed Mexico was ready for democracy. Unlike Díaz, though, Madero truly wished to deliver democracy to the Mexican people.

He was the grandson of Evarista Madero, one of the

JAMES CREELMAN

The interview given by Porfirio Díaz to journalist James Creelman provoked a revolution that resulted in the downfall of his regime. It was not the first time that Creelman's reporting made history.

Creelman was born in Montreal, Canada, in 1859. He left home at the age 13 for New York City, where he received training in the ministry and the law and wrote poetry. At the age of 17, Creelman landed a job at the *New York Herald* and commenced what would become a long career in journalism. During the next few years he traveled across the country, covering the warfare between the feuding Hatfield and McCoy families in the Appalachians and interviewing the Sioux Indian chief Sitting Bull in North Dakota. He soon became a foreign correspondent, and in 1898 covered the Spanish-American War for William Randolph Hearst's *New York Journal.* In Creelman's 1901 book, *On the Great Highway,* he reported Hearst's famous comment to artist Frederic Remington's complaint about being assigned to produce images of fighting in Cuba: "You furnish the pictures and I'll furnish the war."

richest men in Mexico. He would often use his family's wealth to feed hungry Mexicans, whether or not they worked on his grandfather's lands. Francisco Madero was a small, thin man with a high, squeaky voice. He refused to drink alcoholic beverages. Madero hardly looked as though he could fill the role of a strong-willed reformer, but in 1910 he began a candidacy for the presidency. Madero barnstormed across Mexico, shocking Díaz by drawing thousands of listeners to his speeches. This type of campaigning was typical in America but unheard of in Mexico. Obviously, Díaz didn't have a Madero victory in mind when he told *Pearson's Magazine* that Mexico was ready for democracy.

With election day approaching, Díaz concluded that Madero posed a genuine threat to his authoritarian rule. So the old dictator had Madero arrested and thrown into prison. Next, he had the election rigged, declaring himself the winner. On October 4, 1910, the Congress of Mexico met and declared Díaz president for a six-year term. The next day, Díaz released Madero from prison and advised him to leave the country. Madero fled to the United States, where he called on the Mexican people to rise up and overthrow the dictator Porfirio Díaz.

The shooting started in November 1910. The Mexican people proved much harder to fool than Díaz anticipated. They rallied behind charismatic leaders who led uprisings across the country. In the south, thousands of men fell in behind a dynamic rebel leader named Emiliano Zapata. In the north, the state of Chihuahua became one of the major battlefields. Some 3,000 poor Mexicans answered the call to arms and joined a popular, barrel-chested leader who was said to have been a bandit in his youth. His name was Francisco Villa, but everyone knew him by the Mexican nickname for Francisco, "Pancho."

Villa's retirement from the life of a bandit had been all too brief. The 50,000 pesos stolen from the mine owner had quickly slipped through his fingers. Later, Villa claimed to have given most of the money to the poor but, certainly, he surely must have spent some of it on the luxuries of life he never knew as

General Emiliano Zapata, seated center, and his staff in 1912. After Porfirio Díaz rigged the 1910 presidential election, Zapata and other leaders all over Mexico organized uprisings against his regime.

a child. Whatever happened to the money, within 10 months Villa was again broke and found himself returning to the ways of the outlaw.

Soon, though, he grew weary of constantly being on the run and decided to give up the bandit's life to find a job. He made his way to the town of Parral in Chihuahua where he took up a number of occupations, including mining and brick-making. But just when he had settled down to life as an honest laborer, his identity as the notorious bandit Francisco Villa was discovered and he was forced to move on.

Sometime in 1910, Villa met Abraham González, a dynamic and fiery figure in Chihuahua, who told the bandit that times were changing in Mexico. González supported Madero and urged Villa to join the revolution. Villa described González as a "noble martyr for democracy. . .who invited me to fight for the revolution for the rights of the people that had been trampled upon by tyranny. There I understood for the first time that all the suffering, all the hatred, all the rebellion that has accumulated in my soul during so many years of fighting had given me such a strength of conviction and such a clear will that I could offer all this to my country . . . to free her from the snakes that were devouring her entrails."

Villa left his meeting with González a committed member of the rebellion. It is also possible that by 1910, Villa was anxious to become friendly with leaders of a new regime. Certainly, his life as a bandit was bound to catch up with him at some point. In addition to cattle rustling and robbery, Villa was suspected of committing murder. And back in 1901, he had been arrested for the theft of guns and forced by the authorities to join Porfirio Díaz's army. He soon had left the army camp on his own, and so the charge of desertion was hanging over his head as well.

Whether his true motivation was to help the poor and downtrodden Mexicans or to cut himself favorable terms with the new president, the fact remains that Francisco Villa rode into the Chihuahua countryside, and began recruiting men to join the battle against tyranny.

Ten Tragic Days

Fervor for revolution swept through Mexico. Across the nation, impoverished Mexicans joined the rebel leaders and took up arms against Porfirio Díaz. In the southern state of Morelos, a *mestizo* named Emiliano Zapata rode from village to village, recruiting men for the fight. Another *revolucionario* who raised an army was Pascual Orozco Jr. Like Villa, Orozco had been recruited for the cause by Abraham González. The third major military leader to emerge during the early days of the rebellion was Pancho Villa.

After his meeting with González, Villa established a camp in the mountains of Chihuahua. By early October 1910, some 350 men had joined his ragtag group of rebels.

Their first chance to fight came on November 21. Villa and his men rode into the military fort near the Chihuahuan town of San Andrés. It was unoccupied. As the men made themselves at home, Villa learned that a troop train was on its way to San Andrés. Villa

Portrait of General Pancho Villa, ca.1910. As support for the revolution in Mexico steadily increased, Villa attacked multiple Chihuahuan cities with his growing force.

and his men met the train at the station, ambushing the troops as they disembarked from the train.

"*Viva Villa!*" and "*Viva la Revolución!*" the men shouted as they opened fire on the hapless soldiers.

The shooting was over in a few minutes. The *Villistas* killed many soldiers, including the commander of the garrison, while the survivors fled into the countryside. San Andrés was hardly a major victory and it certainly did not show that Villa was a tactical genius or his men fearless fighters; nevertheless, news of the victory over Díaz's troops spread across Mexico. For the first time, rebels had fought soldiers and won. Pancho Villa was now a hero.

Emboldened by the victory at San Andrés as well as other minor skirmishes, Villa now conceived a bold plan. The *Villistas* would attack Ciudad Chihuahua, the state capital. By now, the *Villistas* numbered 500 men. They approached the city and made camp. Villa led about 40 men on a reconnaissance mission. On a hilltop overlooking the city they ran right into a force of 700 federal troops. In a foolish move, Villa's men opened fire, even though they were so greatly outnumbered. Soon, they found themselves in retreat. Villa and his men escaped into the desert and, incredibly, suffered no casualties.

Meanwhile, in Mexico City, Porfirio Díaz resolved to crush the rebellion. Troops were dispatched into the rebellious states. Some 5,000 soldiers were sent into Chihuahua, where fervor for revolution was greatest. At first, it appeared that Díaz's iron-fisted policy would succeed. In Chihuahua, Orozco and his men were defeated at the Battle of Cerro Prieto. Federal troops also kicked the rebels out of the town of Ciudad Guerrero and thwarted their efforts to occupy the cities of Ojinaga and Ciudad Juárez. In early January 1911, rebel leader Apolonio Rodríguez surrendered. Meanwhile, Francisco Madero—the spiritual leader of the revolution—was still in the United States.

Villa was not faring much better. On February 7, the *Villistas* attacked Camargo, which was defended by a garrison of federal troops. Initially, it appeared as though Villa's men would take the town; but just as the battle seemed to be winding down federal reinforcements arrived, forcing the rebels to flee into the countryside. A few days later, the *Villistas* were turned away again when they attacked the town of El Valle de Zaragoza.

Next, Villa planned a siege on Parral, one of the largest cities in Chihuahua. Villa led 150 men into the city to reconnoiter the enemy's positions. Villa had hoped to slip in and out of town quickly, but while moving through the streets of Parral he was recognized and federal troops were alerted. Villa and his men scattered. When he arrived back at his camp in the mountains he found it deserted. Villa caught up with some of the men and learned that survivors of the Parral mission had come back earlier and mistakenly reported that Villa had been killed in a skirmish with federal troops. Disheartened, the men had decided to give up the fight and return to their homes.

But word soon spread that Villa was alive, and by late March some 700 rebels were now riding behind him. Even though the first few months of the war had not gone well for the *revolucionarios*, poor peasants continued to flock to the ranks of Villa and Orozco, as well as Zapata in the south. For the peasants, the rebellion offered hope that their lives would finally improve after so many years of despair and toil on the lands owned by the wealthy *hacendados*. The fact that Villa and the commanders were supplying their armies with horses, food and money stolen in raids on the *haciendas* further endeared the rebel leaders to the peasants, who believed their bloated taskmasters were finally getting what they deserved.

By now, Madero had slipped into Mexico and was taking a personal hand in directing the revolution. Unlike Orozco, who harbored great ambitions to seize the presidency for himself, Villa admired Madero and was anxious to show his loyalty. In March, Villa rode to the town of Bustillos where he met Madero and placed himself and his army under Madero's command.

The Mexico City newspaper *El Tiempo* reported, "This Don Francisco Villa is the man the revolutionaries respect most. While they love and obey Orozco blindly, they fear Villa more, since they know that he will have no inhibition if he wishes to impose his authority. It is said he committed many offenses before he took part in the revolution, but it is stated that since he joined, he has become one of the most honest and incorruptible leaders, who prevents his men from committing offenses."

Madero decided to attack Ciudad Juárez, the second largest city in Chihuahua. Madero was convinced that taking the city could turn the tide of the revolution. The city sits on the southern banks of the Rio Grande River across from El Paso, Texas, and served as an important trade center between the two countries. Indeed, Madero believed that with Ciudad Juárez in rebel hands, he would have a pipeline to arms and other supplies that could be shipped across the river from America. Finally, Madero knew that taking over a city on the doorstep of the United States would show the Americans that the rebels were a force to be reckoned with—a force that the U.S. government should consider supporting.

Madero summoned Villa and Orozco to his headquarters and told them to take Ciudad Juárez. The two leaders headed a combined army of some 1,500 *revolucionarios*. In late April, the rebels launched an attack. Incredibly, they found the city protected by a federal garrison of just 700 troops. The federal soldiers were outnumbered, and all they could do was take up defensive positions. After two days of fighting, Villa and Orozco had the city surrounded, but Madero told them not to make a final assault.

It seemed that Porfirio Díaz wished to talk peace.

For much of the spring things had not been going well in the Mexican capital. Along the Texas border, American troops had mobilized under the orders of President William Howard Taft. U.S. Navy ships also patrolled the Gulf of Mexico. Taft told Mexican diplomats in Washington that the troops and ships were mobilized to stop arms smuggling to the rebels, but Díaz was suspicious of Taft's intentions. This was the era of "jingoism" in American politics: in the United States, political leaders and other men of influence were urging the government of America to exert its will over other countries in the Western Hemisphere. Just 13 years earlier, America had waged war on Spain by invading Cuba. Díaz feared a similar invasion.

And so he sent emissaries to Ciudad Juárez to negotiate terms with Madero. Much to the anger of Villa and Orozco, the rebel leader did not demand Díaz's resignation. Instead, he supported a gradual change of power. Here were Madero's terms: Díaz would be permitted to remain in office for now, but free elections would be scheduled and Díaz would not be permitted to run for a

Revolutionary leader Francisco Madero, seated, and his men headed a revolution in Mexico that led to President Díaz's resignation in 1911. Madero was elected as the next president of Mexico.

new term. Also, Díaz would find a place in his Cabinet for the *revolucionarios*, and the governorships of the Mexican states would also be opened up to opponents of the Díaz government. Those terms were unacceptable to Villa and Orozco because it meant that Díaz would still hold power over the army.

The two rebels refused to live by the terms that Madero had just negotiated. Without telling Madero, the two commanders launched a siege on Ciudad Juárez. The fighting erupted on May 9, 1911. Across the Rio Grande River, Americans standing on rooftops in El Paso could watch the battle. They saw smoke rising from the streets, rebels charging down hillsides, cannons trading fire and the blood of many soldiers spilled.

Madero tried to recall the rebel troops, but by now it was beyond his control. The fighting on the streets of Ciudad Juárez lasted all day and most of the next day as well. Eventually, the rebels overran the outnumbered federal soldiers.

American newspaper correspondent Timothy Turner, who witnessed the fighting, wrote,

> We sat up there on the hill and watched the river oaks swarming with *insurrectos* moving in Juárez. They moved in no formation whatsoever, just an irregular stream of them, silhouettes of men and rifles. Thus they began to move in and to move out along that road throughout the battle. They would fight a while, and come back to rest, sleep and eat, returning refreshed to the front. The European-trained soldiers raved at this, tried to turn them back to make everybody fight at one time. But that was not the way of these chaps from Chihuahua. They knew their business and they knew it well. That way of fighting, I think, more than any other thing, took Juárez. For by it, the *insurrectos* were always fresh with high spirits, while the little brown federals with no sleep and little food or water, with their officers behind them ready with their pistols to kill quitters, soon lost their morale.

Throughout the battle, Pancho Villa fought alongside his men. During one skirmish, Villa and his men made their way to the banks of the Rio Grande River, and then, with Texas at their backs, advanced on the federal troop positions facing the river. The tactics showed a cleverness on Villa's part. He knew the federal troops would be hesitant to shoot toward the river, knowing that errant shots could sail across the Rio Grande and strike Texans watching the battle on the other side. Villa knew that U.S. Army troops were poised to swoop down on Mexico, and he also knew that the federal defenders were under strict orders not to provoke an American invasion. Still, Villa and his men would be running right into the federal guns. This they did bravely, battling their way through the defenses that had been thrown up around the city's perimeter. Throughout the battle, as the *Villistas* advanced on the federal positions, the rebels yelled: *"Viva Mexico! Viva Madero y Villa!"*

What was left of the federal garrison at Ciudad Juárez surrendered to the rebels on May 10, 1911.

The Díaz regime didn't last much longer. At first, Díaz resolved to crush the rebellion. He ordered one of his military commanders, General Victoriano Huerta, to lead a force of soldiers to Ciudad Juárez to oust the rebels. Huerta made plans for the

EMILIANO ZAPATA

Emiliano Zapata assembled an army in the south of Mexico and fought to overthrow Porfirio Díaz. But unlike Pancho Villa, his fellow *revolucionario* in the north, Zapata soon grew suspicious of the new president, Francisco Madero. Indeed, just 11 days after Madero's inauguration as president in November 1911, Zapata broke away and declared a new revolution in the south.

He was born in about 1877 in the state of Morelos and worked as a tenant farmer before joining the revolution in 1910. Indians who toiled as tenant farmers or laborers on *haciendas* across the south flocked to join his army under his battle cry of "Land and Liberty."

Soon after Madero took office, Zapata called for land to be redistributed to poor Indians. When the president indicated no willingness to seize the properties of wealthy Mexican landowners, Zapata staged a series of raids on *haciendas* and sugar plantations in the south. After Madero was arrested and executed, Zapata continued the revolution, opposing Victoriano Huerta. In 1914, he formed an alliance with Villa. Together, the two *revolucionarios* marched on Mexico City and led an uprising against President Venustiano Carranza. In 1919, Zapata was murdered in Morelos by agents dispatched by Carranza.

attack, but other officials in the regime warned the president that, if Huerta marched north, the capital would be left unprotected against the *revolucionarios* in the south led by Emiliano Zapata. And so Díaz ordered Huerta to cancel the expedition.

Now 81 years old and ill from a number of ailments, Díaz decided to simply resign. On May 25, 1911, after 35 years in power, Porfirio Díaz stepped down as president of Mexico. He went to Paris, where he died four years later.

A new election was staged that October, and Francisco Madero was elected president. Alas, the celebration surrounding the end of the despotic regime of Porfirio Díaz and the inauguration of the new reform-minded presidency of Francisco Madero was short-lived. Mexico was a land unaccustomed to democracy, the rule of law and calm. Indeed, Madero faced many problems from the start. Villa had sworn his allegiance to Madero, but few other rebel leaders had done likewise. Most of the rebels were poor and uneducated. Madero, on the other hand, was a member of one of the wealthiest families in Mexico, and for this they mistrusted him. What's more, Madero filled his government with many of his wealthy friends, further infuriating the peasants who had risked their lives fighting against the Díaz regime, believing that they would be treated as equals once the dictator was ousted from power. In the south, Zapata had already started making raids on the large sugar plantations, demanding that the wealthy plantation owners give land grants to the poor Indians. Zapata proclaimed that the new government under Francisco Madero was now his enemy.

Many of the revolutionary leaders distrusted one another as well. Although they fought together for the common cause, Pascual Orozco and Pancho Villa had grown to distrust one another, and would soon become bitter enemies.

Soon after taking office, Madero announced his plans to disarm the rebel army and send the brave *revolucionarios* home, declaring that there was no longer a need for their services. Orozco, for one, was infuriated with Madero's order to disband. He refused to send his troops home and instead led them back

Mexican rebels engaged in civil conflict following Madero's election, when fighting broke out between Villa's and Orozco's armies.

into Chihuahua, vowing to continue the revolution. When Villa refused to join Orozco's force in Chihuahua, Orozco declared him an enemy as well. Meanwhile, other plots were unfolding against the new government. Madero was able to sniff out many of those plots, including the coup that was planned by Félix Díaz.

Troops under Villa and Orozco skirmished from March to June in 1912, until Villa was arrested on Victoriano Huerta's orders. Indeed, Madero had expressed no inclination to purge the new government of troublemakers left over from the Díaz regime. Certainly, he erred by permitting the crafty Victoriano Huerta to remain in a prominent role in the military, which was composed of the same soldiers who fought to protect Díaz from Madero's rebellion. He stood by when Huerta drummed up the phony charges against Villa, had him thrown in prison and nearly executed. And then, suspicious himself of Villa's motives, Madero refused to consider releasing Villa from prison.

Finally, Madero never won over the Americans. U.S. Ambassador Henry Lane Wilson regarded Madero as a weak leader and made it known that he preferred Huerta as president, believing he would bring stability to the region. Wilson's meddling in Mexican politics would mark the beginning of a long and ill-advised policy by U.S. diplomats and intelligence operatives to topple popular regimes in Latin American countries in favor of dictators who, nonetheless, were willing to accept America's friendship. In later years, the United States would have a hand in overthrowing regimes in Nicaragua, Guatemala, and Chile. America's most blatant failure was the botched Bay of Pigs invasion backed by the Central Intelligence Agency in 1961 to topple Cuban communist leader Fidel Castro.

By early 1913, Villa was out of prison, having escaped after serving some seven months. On February 9, 1913, with Pancho Villa hiding in El Paso, a plot unfolded that would result in the arrest, overthrow and assassination of Francisco Madero. This was the beginning of *Decena Tragica*—the "Ten Tragic Days"—one of the darkest chapters in Mexican history.

Although Villa had found a way to escape with the help of Félix Díaz, Díaz continued to languish in the Santiago Tlatelolco military prison. But one morning, a group of soldiers loyal to Díaz overpowered the prison guards and freed the nephew of the former president. Díaz and his followers marched to the presidential palace in Mexico City, where they expected the soldiers guarding President Madero to join the coup. Instead, the garrison remained loyal to Madero, fired on Díaz and killed many of his followers. The few coup participants who survived the siege escaped to an old fort in Mexico City where they took shelter.

That should have been the end of Félix Díaz's uprising, but there were other, more sinister forces at work behind Madero's back. Throughout Mexico, the government wasn't sure how much popular support Díaz may have enjoyed. After all, Zapata and Orozco commanded powerful armies and no one seemed able to guess what they would do next. Villa's men had scattered since his arrest and exile; nevertheless, there were battle-hardened *revolucionarios* sitting in every city and village in Mexico waiting to be called back to arms. Would Pancho Villa come to the aid of Félix Díaz, the man who helped him escape from Santiago Tlatelolco? Could Díaz pose more of a threat than his present circumstances would indicate?

While Díaz and his men hid in the old fort, Wilson urged Huerta to seize the opportunity to overthrow Madero. Huerta consulted Díaz, who agreed to lay down his arms once Madero was removed from power. On February 18, Huerta ordered the arrests of Madero and Vice President Pino Suárez. He promised to spare their lives if they resigned. The two men agreed, and the presidency of Mexico passed into the hands of the usurper, General Victoriano Huerta.

Four days later, Huerta broke his promise to Madero and Suárez. He had them shot.

The Art
of War

While Pancho Villa waged war on Porfirio Díaz's troops in Chihuahua, John Reed was touring Europe to celebrate his graduation from college. He was the son of socially-prominent but far from wealthy parents from Oregon, who nevertheless found the money to send John to prestigious Harvard University in Massachusetts. He graduated in 1910, along with classmates T.S. Eliot, who would become one of America's best-known poets, Walter Lippmann, soon to make his name as a journalist and commentator, and Hamilton Fish Jr., a wealthy New Yorker who would go on to serve in Congress.

When he returned to America, Reed accepted a job offer from muckraking journalist Lincoln Steffens, who had been given Reed's name by a professor at Harvard. Reed settled in New York City and joined the staff of *American Magazine*, which Steffens edited.

While working for *American Magazine*, and later other publications such as *Collier's* and the *Saturday Evening Post*, Reed learned

John Reed, an American journalist, traveled to Mexico in 1914 to cover peasant uprisings. Reed was an advocate of greater rights for oppressed people worldwide, and strongly supported Pancho Villa.

about a different side of American life than he had known at Harvard or in Oregon. He began writing stories about the slum dwellers and others who had not yet tasted their share of the American dream. At Harvard, Reed hadn't paid much attention to politics, but while working as a journalist in New York, Reed found himself drawn to the trade union movement. In 1913, he started writing for *The Masses,* a radical journal whose motto was "to be arrogant, impertinent, in bad taste, but not vulgar . . . to attack old systems, old morals, old prejudices . . . We will be bound by no one creed or theory or social reform, but will express them all, providing they be radical."

As a reporter and editor for *The Masses,* Reed covered a strike by fabric industry workers in Paterson, New Jersey. Reed soon found himself caught up in the strikers' cause and became more than just a reporter covering a story. He marched with the strikers, led them in revolutionary songs and was thrown into jail when, as a result of a Paterson policeman pushing him aside, Reed pushed back.

John Reed's experience in Paterson served to open his eyes to the cause of the oppressed people of the world. In 1914, editors at *Metropolitan* magazine and the *New York World* asked Reed to report on the peasant uprising in Mexico. Reed craved adventure as well as the opportunity to tell the world about a country where poor and oppressed citizens rose up against their wealthy taskmasters. And what better way to tell the story of Mexico than to ride alongside the man who was emerging as the hero of the peasant class: Pancho Villa.

Villa finally made his way from exile in the United States back into Mexico on March 28, 1913, after learning of Madero's assassination and Huerta's seizure of power. He seethed at the image in his mind of Victoriano Huerta presiding over the Mexican people. Other *revolucionarios* were also not happy with Huerta in power. In the south, Emiliano Zapata continued his raids on the *haciendas,* determined to wrest land away from the wealthy class for his peasant followers. Elsewhere, rebel leaders Venustiano Carranza and Alvaro Obregón raised armies as well. Villa added to the tumult when he returned to Chihuahua and recalled his old followers to his ranks.

Finally, the new American president, Woodrow Wilson, opposed Huerta's rule. Wilson concluded that all the Mexican people had accomplished between 1911 and 1913 was to replace one dictator, Porfirio Díaz, with another, Victoriano Huerta. No longer could Huerta count on the support of the American government as he had before.

That was the situation John Reed found in Mexico when he arrived in Chihuahua in 1914 to ride among Pancho Villa's band of rebels.

Reed found a rough-edged man larger than life with a floppy mustache and a personal warmth that made others feel easy and safe in his company. He enjoyed laughing at himself. Reed observed that Villa respected men with education. Villa had, after all, learned to read and write as an adult. He believed strongly in education, and told Reed that once the hostilities ended and stability came to his country, he hoped the new regime would build schools and make education available to all Mexican children.

"Villa's great passion was schools," Reed wrote. "He believed that land for the people and schools would settle every question of civilization . . . Often, I have heard him say: 'When I passed such and such a street this morning I saw a lot of kids. Let's put a school there.'"

Villa adored children and was unable to say no to their demands. He loved to dance, and one time stayed at a friend's wedding for 36 hours because he couldn't pull himself away from the music.

Reed discovered that Villa had a dark side as well. He supported many mistresses and practiced bigamy. Indeed, Villa apparently had two wives. One wife was Juana Torres, a Mexican woman who joined him in El Paso during his exile and remained there when he returned to Chihuahua. The other woman resided in his house in Chihuahua. Her name was Maria Luz Corral de Villa. She married Villa during the uprising against Porfirio Díaz. Their only daughter died at a young age. Villa also fathered many children by other women.

Maria was quite patient with her husband's daliances. "My love for him never diminished," she wrote years later. "I want to firmly state my belief, and this is also my profound conviction, that for a housewife, the love affairs of her husband

Pancho Villa and his wife Maria Luz Corral de Villa at Juárez in 1914.

should be of no importance as long as the wife is loved and respected in her home, which is her sanctuary."

Even Reed, who was brought up in a conservative community in Oregon, could not find fault with Villa. He told his readers,

"Among the *peóns* it is not only not unusual but customary to have more than one mate."

Villa would often dash across the Rio Grande into Texas, where he would see his other wife in El Paso. He enjoyed visiting the bullfight ring and the horseracing track. Good friends who joined him at the racetrack were Tom Mix, the American star of cowboy movies, General Hugh C. Scott, leader of the American troops stationed along the U.S.-Mexico border, and Giuseppe Garibaldi, a descendant of the Italian revolutionary of the same name.

To John Reed, Pancho Villa was a warm-blooded rascal, a star among his people, a lover of women and the last, best hope for a democratic Mexico. But Reed also found a wily, courageous and relentless soldier. Reed wrote: "In all these years he learned to trust nobody. Often in his secret journeys across the country with one faithful companion he camped in some desolate spot and dismissed his guide; then, leaving a fire burning he rode all night to get away from the faithful companion. That is how Villa learned the art of war, and in the field today, when the army comes into camp at night, Villa flings the bridle of his horse to an orderly, takes a serape over his shoulder, and sets out for the hills alone. He never seems to sleep. In the dead of night he will appear somewhere along the line of outposts to see if the sentries are on the job; and in the morning he returns from a totally different direction. No one, not even the most trusted officer on his staff, knows the least of his plans until he is ready for action."

Reed's experiences with Villa would last just a few months. After returning to the United States, Reed found himself drifting more and more toward socialism. In 1917 he traveled to Russia to witness the Bolshevik revolution. His reporting of the revolution in the book *Ten Days that Shook the World* is regarded as the most vivid eyewitness account of the upheaval that led to the establishment of the Soviet Union. He died in 1920 in Russia. Bolshevik leaders ordered that his ashes be interred in the wall of the Kremlin, the building that served as the seat of government for the Soviet Union and now Russia. Although he advocated a political philosophy that would be doomed for extinction by the end of the 20th century, there is no question that first in Mexico and then in Russia, John Reed believed in the right of the oppressed masses to rise up against the wealthy and privileged few.

The fight was now against Victoriano Huerta. Villa had many reasons to want Huerta dead. Certainly, his false imprisonment and near execution at the hands of the usurper were reason enough, but Huerta was also responsible for the murder of Abraham González, Villa's mentor and the governor of Chihuahua. Villa struck an alliance with rebel leader Venustiano Carranza, the self-proclaimed "First Chief of the Revolution" and, in fact, placed his army at Carranza's disposal. Although in public Villa referred to Carranza as the *jefe*—in English, the "leader"—in private, Villa confided his hatred for Carranza. He told friends, "I embraced him energetically, but with the first few words we spoke, my blood turned to ice. I saw that I could not open my heart to him. He never looked me in the eye and during our entire conversation emphasized our differences in origin . . . lectured me on things like decrees and laws which I could not understand. There was nothing in common between that man and me." Indeed, Villa regarded Carranza as soft yet ambitious and not dedicated to the plight of the peasants. Zapata was suspicious of Carranza as well.

Likewise, Carranza felt little love for Villa. He believed Villa to be ambitious. Confiding to friends, he once claimed: "He is a terrible man, and a man without any visions, someone who is not conscious of what he is doing; he is enormously dangerous and we must be prepared." Villa further infuriated Carranza when he declared himself governor of Chihuahua. Carranza, who had few political allies in the vast northern state, realized now that he would never command complete obedience from the *revolucionarios* in Chihuahua.

And so, both men only grudgingly accepted this rocky alliance. Villa enjoyed considerable military success, defeating

Huerta's federal troops in several battles during the first five months of 1914. By now, Villa commanded 8,000 rebel troops in what was known as the *Division del Norte*—the Division of the North. His army swept through not only Chihuahua but nearby states as well. In the state of Coahuilo, Villa's men overran garrisons in the towns of Paredon and Saltillo, defeating federal troops numbering some 6,000 men.

On February 17, 1914, Villa found himself in a squabble with William S. Benton, a British citizen and owner of a Chihuahua *hacienda*. Benton sold cattle to Villa and went to Villa's home to collect the money that was owed him. The argument over the debt turned out to be quite brief—Villa ended it by shooting

AMBROSE BIERCE

John Reed isn't the only American author to have ridden with Pancho Villa. Ambrose Bierce, a journalist and author of darkly satirical stories, joined Villa's troops in 1913. Unlike Reed, who would go on to further adventures, Bierce disappeared while in Mexico. Some historians believe he was murdered on Villa's orders.

He was born in 1842 in Ohio and served in the Union Army during the Civil War. Following the war, Bierce headed west and settled in San Francisco, where he found a job as a newspaper reporter. By 1872 he was living in London, where he authored his first book of satire, *Cobwebs from an Empty Skull*.

He returned from London, found work with American newspapers, and in 1913 traveled to Mexico to ride with Villa, who called him "Old Gringo." Unlike Reed, who regarded Villa as a hero, Bierce described Villa and his men as a "band of assassins who did not respect anything or anyone." And then he made the mistake of telling Villa that he planned to join the forces of rebel leader Venustiano Carranza, whom Villa was growing to hate.

According to legend, Villa embraced Bierce, wished him well and sent him on his way into the Chihuahua Desert, only to be shot dead by men carrying out Villa's orders.

Benton. Later, Villa claimed he shot Benton in self-defense, but the furor over the killing soon became an international incident. The British government insisted that Villa was a bloodthirsty bandit, unfit to lead a revolution whose aim was establishing democracy in Mexico.

The killing of Benton placed President Woodrow Wilson in a touchy diplomatic corner. Just 16 days before the shooting, Wilson had withdrawn the embargo on arms shipments to the rebels. It was an enormous diplomatic victory for the *revolucionarios*, who could now obtain guns, cannons and ammunition from American suppliers in the war against Huerta. But with Great Britain—America's close ally—accusing Pancho Villa of the cold-blooded murder of a British citizen, it appeared that America's support for the rebels could be short-lived. Some deft diplomatic maneuvering, clearly beyond the capabilities of the hot-headed Villa, was needed.

It was Venustiano Carranza who stepped in to defuse the tempers of the British diplomats. Carranza appointed a commission to investigate the shooting, which declared that Benton lived in Mexico for 30 years and had become a naturalized Mexican citizen and, therefore, Pancho Villa could not be held responsible for the murder of a British citizen. What's more, Benton was shown to be a vicious and brutal *hacendado* who abused his Mexican *peóns*, often whipping them. The British fumed, but the whole matter was soon forgotten. Carranza's handling of the Benton affair impressed President Wilson. As for Villa, he escaped from the incident with another dent in his already tarnished reputation.

On April 9, 1914, troops serving under Victoriano Huerta committed a diplomatic blunder that would help lead to Huerta's resignation as president. The American battleship USS *Dolphin* had been stationed off the coast of the Mexican port city of Tampico. That night, nine sailors were sent ashore to obtain gasoline. While obtaining the fuel in Tampico, they were arrested.

The Mexicans held them for just an hour, then released the men. When word of the incident reached the White House,

Woodrow Wilson used it to denounce the Huerta government. He demanded a formal apology from Huerta, including a 21-gun salute. Huerta, in return, demanded a 21-gun salute from the decks of the *Dolphin*. The two sides were at a stalemate.

On April 21, Wilson found his excuse to invade Mexico. The German ship *Ypirango* arrived off the coastal town of Veracruz with an arms shipment for Huerta's troops. Ostensibly to keep the arms out of Huerta's hands—but really to destabilize the Mexican government—Wilson ordered American Marines to invade Veracruz.

The Americans found little resistance. Huerta's troops fled the town rather than battle American soldiers. Veracruz's defenders included some civilians and naval cadets, who were swept aside in short order. In Washington, Secretary of War Lindley M. Garrison urged Wilson to reinforce the landing party in Veracruz and send the Marines right into Mexico City. While Wilson did send more soldiers into Veracruz, they were told to stay put at first.

Meanwhile, the rebels advanced. On June 23, 1914, Villa's men took the town of Zacatecas. On July 8, rebels under Alvaro Obregón captured Guadalajara.

On July 15, with rebel armies in overwhelming numbers advancing on Mexico City, President Victoriano Huerta resigned and fled the country. In the months that followed, Venustiano Carranza would emerge as the new president of Mexico.

Wilson found Carranza as hard to deal with as Huerta. Carranza demanded that the U.S. troops withdraw from Veracruz. Wilson stalled, but after three months of constant prodding the American president finally gave the withdrawal order. With the Americans now off Mexican soil, Carranza made it clear that America's interests were now subordinate to Mexico's. Carranza declared that all oil and mineral rights would be reserved for the Mexican people. Mexico was (and still is) an important supplier of the world's oil, and even in the early 1900s American oil companies had invested heavily in Mexico to develop the country's petroleum industry. Now, the First Chief

On April 21, 1914, U.S. president Woodrow Wilson ordered troops to invade the Mexican town Veracruz. Several months later, Mexican president Victoriano Huerta (pictured here) resigned his position and fled the country.

was threatening to seize those assets. Wilson was enraged.

"I have never known a man more impossible to deal with," declared Wilson.

Meanwhile, the *revolucionario* leaders in the countryside continued the civil war. Villa hated Carranza, and so did Zapata. They sent their men on raids against federal troops.

In any war, innocent civilians are often caught in the crossfire. In this war, about 170 Americans who made their homes below the Rio Grande had already lost their lives. Wilson advised Americans to leave Mexico and return to the United States. During 1915, some 40,000 Americans left the country.

With war again raging in Mexico, Wilson had no choice but to recognize Carranza as the president of the country. Although he despised Carranza, Wilson believed the First Chief was the only one who could return calm to the country. And so the American president grudgingly extended recognition and aid to Carranza's government.

On November 1, 1915, Villa threw his *revolucionarios* into an assault on federal troops at Agua Prieta, just south of the American border town of Douglas, Arizona. The battle proved a disaster for Villa. Four times his cavalry soldiers charged the well-defended fort, and four times they were repelled. Hundreds of *revolucionarios* died in the attack. Villa blamed America for his defeat. With Wilson extending diplomatic relations to Carranza, the First Chief was able to send reinforcements and supplies to Agua Prieta from the north. Indeed, the Mexican soldiers had crossed over into the United States, boarded trains in Arizona, and then rode to the rescue of their *compadres* in Aqua Prieta. Villa's men had no permission to cross over into America and, therefore, could do nothing to stem the flow of reinforcements.

General Hugh Scott had warned Wilson against permitting Carranza's troops the use of American railroads to outmaneuver Villa. He wrote, "We permitted Carranza to send his troops through the United States by our rails to crush Villa. I did what I could to prevent this."

Scott added that Wilson had made Villa an outlaw and predicted that the wild and unpredictable rebel leader would find a way to take his revenge on the United States.

Raid on Columbus

The first hint of what was to come materialized on January 10, 1916, when a train heading to the Chihuahua mining town of Cusihuiriáchic was stopped by a detachment of Villa's troops. On board were 19 American mining engineers who had fled Chihuahua some months before, but were now returning because they believed the country had stabilized.

They were wrong. The *Villistas* boarded the train near the town of Santa Isabel and executed the Americans on the spot. Only one American, Thomas B. Holmes, escaped from the carnage. He had gotten off the train when the *revolucionarios* brought it to a halt, and managed to escape by jumping into some bushes when the shooting started. Another traveller, Cesar Sala, an Italian, was permitted to live because of his nationality. He said that a *Villista* leveled a gun at him, called him a *gringo* and prepared to fire.

Sala recalled: "I told him I was not an American and said, 'I am not a *gringo*.' He then told me to sit down and cursed the president

When President Woodrow Wilson acknowledged Carranza as president of Mexico, he angered Villa. Villa and his men responded with attacks on American soil.

of the United States and Mr. Carranza and said they were after the Americans."

Other witnesses reported that the *Villistas* wanted to rob the Mexican passengers on the train, but their leader, Colonel Pablo López, had forbidden them from doing so, telling his men that they were just there to kill Americans.

Over the next several weeks the *Villistas* skirmished openly with American troops along the border. Villa's men also attacked

American-owned ranches and mining companies throughout Chihuahua. In the United States, political leaders and other influential citizens called on President Wilson to protect American interests in Mexico and bring the Santa Isabel killers to justice. Nearly two decades before, newspapers owned by William Randolph Hearst and Joseph Pulitzer pushed the American government into invading Cuba. Now, the press advocated an invasion of Mexico.

"We are too proud to fight," complained Hearst's *Los Angeles Examiner*. "Why, even a little, despicable, contemptible bandit nation like Mexico murders our citizens, drags our flags in the dirt and spits and defies this nation of ours with truculent insolence."

But Wilson refused to intercede, explaining that since the attack on the Santa Isabel train had occurred on Mexican soil, it was a matter for the Mexican government to handle.

Following his defeat at Agua Prieta, Villa's once-formidable army had dwindled down to a force of just a few hundred dedicated men. The assaults on Carranza's troops had cost hundreds of lives. Many other men deserted Villa's ranks. After five years of civil war, they were weary and wanted only to return home to pick up their lives.

Perhaps even Villa realized that his days as a great rebel leader were near the end. He gathered his remaining men and told them his aim was to attack the border towns in Texas, Arizona and New Mexico to make America pay for its support for Carranza's troops at Agua Prieta.

"Large detachments of our troops will join us en route," he promised his soldiers. "I shall hold none of you after that venture, and I assure you that you will not regret participating in this last expedition with me."

On March 1, 1916, a Villa raiding party arrived at a ranch in Chihuahua, owned by American E.J. Wright and his wife Maud. The Wrights, and a friend by the name of Hayden, were taken prisoner. After a few days of hard riding, Hayden and E.J. Wright were taken into the countryside and murdered. When Maud Wright asked the head of the raiding party, Colonel Nicolás Hernández, whether she would also be killed, he told her that Villa intended to take her to the town of Columbus, New Mexico. When the woman asked Hernández what Villa wanted in Columbus, he replied, "To burn and loot the town and kill every American there."

During the ride north, Maud Wright made many appeals to the *Villistas* to free her. She was even granted an audience with Pancho Villa himself, but the rebel leader refused. "Villa intends for you to die a horrible death," Hernández told the American

WAS GERMANY BEHIND THE RAID ON COLUMBUS?

After Pancho Villa's raid on Columbus, New Mexico, many people believed the German government may have had a hand the attack.

World War I had been raging in Europe since 1914. German leaders were concerned that America would soon enter the war on the side of the British and French, or at least would supply its allies with weapons and supplies.

Was it possible that German agents encouraged Villa to raid an American town, specifically to provoke an American invasion of Mexico? With American troops and supplies tied up in a long campaign in Mexico, the United States would be in no position to aid its allies in Europe.

There was plenty of evidence to suggest German involvement. It is known that the Germans first approached Victoriano Huerta, who was by then hiding in America, and offered him $10 million to return to Mexico, raise an army and attack the United States. Also, Felix Sommerfeld, a German soldier of fortune closely allied with Villa, often boasted that he could prompt the rebel leader into attacking the United States. Throughout the early months of 1916, Sommerfeld communicated with German diplomats, and is believed to have supplied arms to the *Villistas*. But it should be pointed out that Pancho Villa's hatred for President Woodrow Wilson was so strong at this point that he probably needed no prompting from a foreign power to wage war on America.

woman at one point. "You will ride day and night until we reach Columbus—if you live that long."

On March 8, a force of 400 *Villistas* arrived just south of the New Mexico town of Columbus. This time, Pancho Villa was at the head of the column.

Columbus was a curious choice by Villa to stage a raid. It was a small town of just a few hundred people, many who scratched out their livings as farmers. About 600 troops of the U.S. Army's 13th Cavalry were stationed at Camp Furlong, just south of the town. Had Villa known the garrison was that large, it is unlikely he would have selected Columbus for the attack. But Villa's spies provided him with poor information, reporting that only some 50 U.S. Army soldiers protected the town.

Just before 5 A.M. on the morning of March 9, Villa and his men laid siege to Columbus, New Mexico. It was the first time since British troops invaded the United States during the War of 1812 that a foreign army attacked American citizens on American soil.

Villa sent half his men to Camp Furlong, where they surprised the American troops sleeping in their barracks. Villa found far more men than the 50 troops his spies told him to expect, but the *Villistas* still outnumbered the Americans. About 400 American soldiers had been dispatched a few days before to nearby ranches in anticipation of *Villista* attacks.

"*Viva Villa! Viva Mexico! Muerte a los americanos!*" the *Villistas* shouted as they swept through the Army camp.

Only the cooks were awake when the shooting started. They rose first to prepare breakfast for the garrison and were brewing coffee when the raiders entered the camp. The cooks found themselves in the unusual position of being the first line of defense for their garrison, yet they responded well to the challenge, heaving boiling kettles of coffee at the *Villistas* and blasting away at them with the heavy and awkward shotguns they usually used to hunt game. Elsewhere in the camp, the startled American soldiers protected themselves as best they could, but were soon low on ammunition. Also, two of the garrison's four machine guns jammed. Still, they put up a good fight. Lieutenant W. A. McCain killed one of the attackers with the butt of his pistol. Another Mexican was knocked off his horse by a soldier wielding a baseball bat. At Camp Furlong, the *Villistas* lost far more men than they expected.

Meanwhile, the other half of Villa's army swept through Columbus. James Dean, the owner of Lemmon & Romnet, the town's grocery store, had the misfortune of walking down Main Street in order to open the store, when the raiding party hit town. He was among the first to die. The store itself was set afire by the raiders, who poured gallons of kerosene throughout the building and then ignited the blaze with a match. At the town hardware store, the *Villistas* smashed the windows and stole saddles and other supplies before they set that store on fire as well.

Several *Villista* raiders entered the Commercial Hotel where they roused startled guests from their sleep, robbing some of them and killing others. Hotel guest Walton R. Walker was jerked away from his wife and shot to death before her eyes. Dr. H. M. Hart, a veterinarian, and Charles De Witt Miller, an engineer, were pushed into the street, robbed and murdered. The owner of the hotel, William T. Ritchie, huddled in fright with his wife and three daughters. The raiders found him, shoved him into the street and shot him down. Before leaving, they ripped the gold wedding band from his widow's finger.

Other women and children were also unfortunate victims. A 16-year-old boy named Arthur Ravel was abducted off the street by two Mexicans, but was saved by sure-sighted towns-people who picked off the *Villista* kidnappers from the safety of sniper posts. Mrs. Milton James, the wife of a railroad worker, wasn't as fortunate. She was killed in a volley of gunfire.

Maud Wright escaped from Villa's men during the raid. At some point during the battle, she slipped away and hid in a ditch. For a time she believed she was safe, but was spotted by a Mexican on horseback. It was Villa. She looked into the eyes

Men from the 13th U.S. Cavalry find a dead Villa raider. The *Villistas* attacked Columbus, New Mexico, in 1916, but found numerous American soldiers waiting to strike.

of the rebel leader and begged him to let her go. Villa nodded curtly and rode off.

As dawn approached the raid drew to an end. Seventeen Americans had been killed in the raid on Columbus. About 40 more were wounded. The *Villistas* lost about 120 men, many of them killed by American troops from the 13th Cavalry, who chased them back into Mexico. Indeed, the Americans rode five miles into Mexico in pursuit of the *Villistas*, but were driven back when Villa's men suddenly stopped, running to make a stand.

Back in the United States, the *Villistas* raid on Columbus prompted outrage throughout the country. Newspapers reported that *Villistas* captured after the raid told American authorities that Pancho Villa instructed them to burn and loot the town and make "human torches" of every man, woman and child they found. In New Mexico, innocent Mexicans suspected of spying for the *Villistas* were arrested and questioned. After their release, six of them were murdered by Americans seeking revenge. In

Mexico, President Carranza guaranteed the safety of all Americans; nevertheless, hundreds of Americans boarded trains to leave the country.

Wilson found himself under considerable pressure from Congress and the press to respond to the attack. "Nothing less than Villa's life can atone for this outrage," declared Joseph Pulitzer's *New York World*.

Pulitzer's rival, William Randolph Hearst, went further. His newspapers advocated American occupation of Mexico as well as other Latin American countries.

"California and Texas were part of Mexico once," fumed an editorial in a Hearst paper. "What has been done in California and Texas by the United States can be done all the way down to the southern bank of the Panama Canal and beyond."

It was March 1916. Wilson was up for re-election that fall. A second term was not at all assured. Wilson knew that he could no longer rely on Venustiano Carranza to rein in Villa, and that he would have to send an expeditionary force into Mexico to track down the rebel leader. And so he committed the United States to an invasion of Mexico.

"It is not a difficult thing for a president to declare war, especially against a weak and defenseless nation like Mexico," Wilson said. He added:

> Men forget what is back of the struggle in Mexico. It is the age-long struggle of the people to come into their own, and while we look upon the incidents in the foreground, let us not forget the tragic reality in the background which towers above the whole sad picture. The gentlemen who criticize me speak as if America were afraid to fight Mexico. Poor Mexico with its pitiful men, women and children fighting to gain a foothold in their own land.

6

The Punitive Expedition

Since graduating from the U.S. Military Academy at West Point in 1882, John J. Pershing had put together a stellar Army career. He was first sent to New Mexico and Arizona, where he fought in cavalry units battling the last remaining warriors of the Apache nation under Geronimo. During the Spanish-American War, Pershing participated in the battle of San Juan Hill. He also fought in the Philippines, served as a diplomat in Japan and held several teaching assignments. In the military, Pershing was known as "Black Jack." He earned his nickname in the 1890s while serving as an officer in the 10th Cavalry, which was composed mostly of African American soldiers.

By 1916, Pershing had risen to the rank of brigadier general. On March 10, 1916, just one day after Pancho Villa's raid on Columbus, Pershing was chosen to head what would become known as the "Punitive Expedition."

Despite the urgings of the Hearst and Pulitzer newspapers,

General John Pershing was selected in 1916 to head the "Punitive Expedition," an attempt by the United States to capture Pancho Villa.

Wilson did not want to wage war on Mexico. To do so would have meant fighting against President Venustiano Carranza's army on many fronts. Certainly, there was no question that America enjoyed a vast military might over Mexico, but Wilson had no taste for a long and, most likely, unpopular occupation of Mexico. After all, Mexicans had been waging bloody civil war since 1910; there was no reason to risk American lives with the likes of Pancho Villa and Emiliano Zapata roaming the hills.

And so, on the morning of March 10, President Wilson announced:

> An adequate force will be sent at once in pursuit of Villa with the single object of capturing him and putting a stop to his forays. This can and will be done in entirely friendly aid to the constitutional authorities in Mexico and with scrupulous respect for the soverignty of that republic.

Well, not quite. In Mexico City, the First Chief seethed at the idea of American troops rolling through the Mexican countryside. It was true that Carranza had no love for Pancho Villa; nevertheless, he vehemently opposed the Punitive Expedition, arguing that his own troops could track down Villa and bring him to justice. On March 12, newspapers in Mexico City carried a statement from the president, warning that Mexico "would not admit under any circumstances and whatever may be the reasons advanced and the explanations offered by the government of the United States about the act it proposes to carry out, that the territory of Mexico be invaded for an instant and the dignity of the Republic outraged."

The two sides seemed teetering on the edge of war. Carranza moved his troops to the border and positioned them to repel an American invasion, while in New Mexico, some 5,000 U.S. Army troops amassed and prepared to cross the border. Telegrams flew back and forth between diplomats in Washington, D.C., and Mexico City. And then, suddenly, on the morning of March 15— just hours before Pershing's troops were scheduled to cross the border—the U.S. State Department received a telegram from diplomats stationed in Columbus. The Mexican Army commander at the border notified the Americans that he was ordered to stand aside and permit the Punitive Expedition to cross. Carranza had changed his mind. There would be no war with the United States.

It is likely that Pancho Villa would have greatly enjoyed watching his two most bitter enemies, Wilson and Carranza, rattle their sabers at one another. But Villa was too busy making his getaway. In just a few hours he had transformed himself from an grumpy rebel into the world's most wanted man. By now, there were fewer than 200 *revolucionarios* under his command. Soon, some 5,000 American troops would be on his trail. U.S. Army airplanes flew over the Chihuahua mountains, searching for signs of the rebel force. In the Gulf of Mexico, the battleship USS *Kentucky* dropped anchor just off the coast from Veracruz. And, certainly, Carranza's men were looking for him as well.

The *Villistas* suffered huge losses in the raid on Columbus. The many wounded men that they had to carry with them slowed their retreat into the mountains. In the ranks of the raiders, there was talk of mass desertion. But Villa was still a charismatic and popular commander among his men, some of whom had been following him for six years. He held the ranks together and made plans for their escape.

Word of the raid on Columbus quickly spread through the

GEORGE S. PATTON

Lieutenant George S. Patton was a young officer assigned to duty on the Punitive Expedition. In later years, Patton would attain the rank of general and serve as an important leader during World War II. He would become known by the nickname "Blood and Guts" for his hard-charging tactics.

Patton was born into a wealthy family and, as a boy, became an expert horseman and student of history. He graduated from the United States Military Academy at West Point, New York, in 1909. He served as an aide on General John J. Pershing's staff during the Punitive Expedition.

Patton was involved in many battles in Mexico and killed a *Villista* in a gun battle at a ranch near the town of Rubio. After the battle, he wrote to his wife: "You are probably wondering if my conscience hurts me for killing a man. It does not. I feel about it just as I did when I got my first swordfish: surprised at my luck."

Mexican countryside. On March 14, the *Villistas* arrived in the town of Galeana. They were surprised to find that several thousand Mexicans had gathered to catch a glimpse of the brave rebel leader who had challenged the *gringos*.

Villa stopped in town long enough to make a speech. He told them:

> Brethren, I have called you together to inform you that in an endeavor to enter the United States I was stopped by the *gringos* on the line and was compelled to fight large numbers of them. I repeat to you, I shall not waste one more cartridge on our Mexican brothers but will save all my ammunition for the 'blonds.' Prepare yourselves for the fight that is to come.

Villa asked the people of Galeana to care for his wounded. The Mexican citizens happily complied, and also showered his men with food, clothes, money and ammunition. As the *Villistas* rode on, they found citizens in other towns just as willing to help. Across northern Mexico, peasants learned the words to this song:

> Maybe they have guns and cannons,
> Maybe they are a lot stronger,
> We have only rocks and mountains -
> But we know how to last longer.

The chase was on! Pershing ordered his men to cross the border at 11 A.M. on March 15, splitting them into two forces that would take separate routes south. They were led by cowboys, Apache Indians and local desperados who signed on as scouts. A reporter for the *San Francisco Bulletin* described the departure of the troops: "A long hazy line of alkali dust, standing out against the dull white of the plains and the blazing light of the sun, marked their progress toward the border as viewed from a hill above the village."

President Carranza led U.S. and Mexican troops on a search along the railroad tracks for Villa bandits. The troops tracked down Villa's men just days after the Americans crossed into Mexico, but the *Villistas* defeated them.

Pershing brought four cavalry regiments, two infantry regiments and two artillery units into Mexico. The artillery units were armed with eight cannons as well as machine guns and howitzers. Some of the cannons were powerful enough to launch a shot some three miles. Also making the trek were engineers, ambulance companies and the Signal Corps. It took so long for the two columns to cross into Mexico that General Pershing himself didn't cross the border until shortly after midnight on March 16. And just as Carranza's commander had promised, the Mexican troops offered no resistance to the columns of American soldiers.

While there may have been no resistance by the Mexicans, there was no help from them, either. Whenever the troops would arrive in a Chihuahuan town, the local residents refused to provide information on the whereabouts of the *Villistas*. Two weeks into the mission, Pershing wired his first telegraph message back to America: "Our troops seem to be pressing him, but I won't hazard any predictions. Villa is no fool—it may be that the campaign has just started."

It was Carranza's men who caught up with Villa first. On March 17, a Mexican army regiment attacked Villa. The *Villistas* quickly escaped. Ten days later they arrived at the town of Ciudad Guerrero, where they defeated Carranza's troops, captured a large cache of arms, and even persuaded some 80 federal soldiers to join their ranks. During the fighting, though, Villa was shot in the knee.

The rebel leader was in great pain and clearly unable to ride at the head of his troops. So he split them into small detachments and sent them into the mountains to hide. Then, protected by a small bodyguard of a few dedicated men, Villa made his way to a ranch owned by the father of one of his officers. Villa spent several days hiding at the ranch to recover from his leg wound.

Pershing and his men pressed on. The Mexican countryside was rugged, bleak and unforgiving. Despite all the resources available to the Punitive Expedition, the men were often hungry and there never seemed to be enough water to drink. Many of the mules that carried equipment or pulled the heavy cannons died on the trail. The men were constantly exhausted from their long hours of marching. Soon, the American troops lost the use of the eight biplanes that had been used for aerial reconnaissance. Only five weeks after the expedition commenced, all eight of the planes crashed or were grounded due to a lack of replacement parts.

In early April, Pershing dispatched Major Frank Tompkins to Parral with infantry and cavalry troops on a hunch that Villa was hiding there. But instead of finding Villa and his men in Parral, Tompkins encountered a garrison of hostile

Carranza troops. Soon, firing broke out between the two sides. It is estimated that 40 Mexican soldiers were killed, while the Americans suffered only two casualties. Back home, newspapers reporting the incident couldn't help but point out that in the first skirmish of the Punitive Expedition, the American soldiers traded gunfire with troops who were supposed to have been their friends.

On May 11, the U.S. Army finally engaged the *Villistas*. At the Ojos Azules Ranch, an American garrison came upon a band of Villa's men snoozing in the bunkhouse. The Americans launched an assault on the ranch in the early morning hours. The raid on Ojos Azules lasted just 20 minutes. The Americans claimed to have killed 42 *Villistas* at the ranch and another 19 in the hills shortly after the raid. Pancho Villa was not among the rebels killed or captured.

Such victories by Pershing's troops were rare. By the start of the summer, the general still had no idea where he could find Pancho Villa. His men were bogged down, fighting off relentless Mexican flies, blinding desert sandstorms, freezing nights in the Sierra Madres, and roads that turned into knee-deep muddy bogs following a rainstorm. In Washington, President Wilson's aides worried that America would soon be drawn into the war in Europe and that Pershing's men would be needed overseas. They told Wilson that the whole Punitive Expedition was turning out to be a waste of time and resources. Indeed, Secretary of War Newton Baker concluded that Pershing would never find Villa. He believed that the Americans had performed their duty by dispersing Villa's men, and thus had made sure that they were no longer a threat to American citizens. General Hugh Scott, Villa's former friend from his racetrack days, was now U.S. Army chief of staff. He said, "I do not know how long this thing is going to continue. It seems to me that Pershing has accomplished all that he was sent for. It does not seem dignified for all the United States to be hunting for one man in a foreign country. If the thing were reversed, we would not allow any foreign army to be

President Carranza led the troops to capture the *Villistas* during the Punitive Expedition. Carranza's troops faced trouble after the American government placed another arms embargo on Mexico.

sloshing around in our country, 300 miles from the border, no matter who they were."

But Wilson decided to keep the expedition in Mexico, and the hunt continued.

By now, Villa had recovered from his leg wound and was on the move again. Word of his recovery spread throughout Chihuahua, and many of his men rejoined his army. Indeed, the *Villista* ranks swelled to several thousand *revolucionarios*. In the eyes of the poor Chihuahuan people, Villa remained a hero. Their lives had not improved under President Carranza, and they despised him for failing to drive the Americans out of their country.

They regarded Villa as far braver than the Carranza generals. And Carranza's icy relations with the American government didn't help his popularity, either. Following the Columbus raid, Wilson had again slapped an arms embargo on Mexico, making it hard for Carranza to supply his troops with guns and ammunition. To make sure his soldiers had weapons and ammunition, Carranza established his own munitions factories. But Villa seemed to have no difficulty obtaining what he needed from the factories, or even from the Carranza soldiers themselves when his men defeated them in battle. In addition, his old friend Felix Sommerfeld was making sure German arms found their way into the hands of his troops, smuggling them past border guards using ludicrous methods of camouflage, such as hiding the guns in coffins.

Meanwhile, the American and Mexican troops seemed more interested in keeping wary eyes on one another than in searching for Villa. There seemed to be constant skirmishes between the Americans and the Carranza soldiers. On June 21, both sides suffered heavy losses during a gun battle in the town of Carrizal. Twenty-three Americans were taken prisoner at Carrizal, although they were released within a few days.

Now that his men were well armed, rested, and had replenished their supplies, Villa decided it was time to start fighting back. Over the summer, his men committed a series of guerilla raids on Carranza's troops in Chihuahua and neighboring Durango. On September 15 — Mexico's

Independence Day—he launched an offensive on Ciudad Chihuahua, the state capital. Villa led 2,000 men into the town, where they found the Carranza soldiers had let down their guards in celebration of the national holiday. *Villistas* freed hundreds of political prisoners from the Ciudad Chihuahua jail, many of whom had been condemned to death and were eager to join his ranks. Following the quick raid, the *Villistas* fled into the mountains.

Pancho Villa moved quickly to attack other towns, never tasting defeat until his men rode into the village of Santa Isabel. The village was unguarded. Foolishly, the rebels failed to post sentries while they celebrated their easy victory. Federal troops soon arrived and engaged the *Villistas* in battle; at first, the government troops held the upper hand and drove them out of town. But the next day Villa's men regrouped, staged a new assault on Santa Isabel and this time won the day.

By late fall, although Pershing's men had conducted small skirmishes with the *Villistas*, the main force of the general's army had failed to confront Villa's army in a major assault. What's more, Villa had escaped from Columbus in March with just 200 rebels under his command. Now, he found himself at the head of a formidable fighting force of several thousand peasant soldiers. Meanwhile, Wilson was convinced that Germany aimed to widen the war that had been raging in Europe. In just a few months, the Germans would start attacking neutral shipping in the Atlantic Ocean. Wilson knew he would need the troops for service in Europe. In fact, on April 6, 1917, America would declare war on the Central Powers and enter World War I. General Pershing would be selected to head the American Expeditionary Force, which departed for France a few months later.

After several weeks of negotiations, the Americans reached terms with Carranza's government for withdrawal of the Punitive Expedition from Mexico. The withdrawal commenced on January 28, 1917, and was completed eight days later.

General Pershing, for one, believed the Punitive Expedition had served its purpose. He wrote in his memoirs:

> After we had penetrated about 400 miles into Mexican territory . . . the increasing disapproval of the Mexican government doubtless caused the administration to conclude that it would be better to rest content that the outlaw bands had been severely punished and generally dispersed, and that the people of northern Mexico had been taught a salutary lesson.

Although Villa successfully escaped from Pershing's net, many other leaders of his rebel army were not so fortunate. Several of his officers had been caught or killed in the weeks following the Columbus raid. In the United States, newspaper readers were delighted to read of the news that Carranza's men had captured Pablo López, who ordered the massacre of the American mining engineers at Santa Isabel. López had been wounded at Columbus. Following the raid, he limped into Chihuahua, where he hid in the mountains. He was tracked down by federal troops. Weary, wounded and without food or water for three days, López surrendered.

López was jailed in Ciudad Chihuahua and sentenced to death. On May 16, 1916, he gave an interview to a reporter for the *El Paso Herald*. During the interview, López admitted that he ordered the murders of the American mining engineers. López stated boldly:

> I would much prefer to die for my country in battle, but if it is decided to kill me, I will die as Pancho Villa would wish me to—with my head erect and my eyes unbandaged and history will not be able to record that Pablo López flinched on the brink of eternity.

A few days after, Pablo López stood in front of a firing squad. He refused a blindfold and gave the order to fire himself.

7

Death of a Rebel

For the next three years, Pancho Villa continued his relentless guerrilla campaign against President Carranza's federal troops. "As I do not see the slightest hope of a change of conduct on the part of the men in power in the country, I have the honor to state to the Mexican people that, from this time on, I shall push military operations as far as possible in order to overthrow the traitors and place at the head of the government the citizen who, through his recognized honor and civic virtues, shall cause Mexico to figure in the catalogue of civilized and free peoples, which is the place legitimately belonging to her," Villa told the Mexican people in a manifesto he issued in late 1916.

Villa always maintained that he held no ambitions for power himself. Three years earlier, he told John Reed, "I am a fighter, not a statesman." Indeed, he was determined to remain a fighter as long as Venustiano Carranza remained in power. During this period, the conflict turned far more vicious than it had been since

General Villa participated in guerilla warfare against President Carranza's troops after Pershing and his troops withdrew. Villa's campaign grew more violent as his troops began attacking innocent civilians and towns.

the revolution to oust Porfirio Díaz commenced some seven years before. Prisoners were executed, stores and ranches were looted and innocent civilians were murdered. In 1920, journalists reported the shocking news that Pancho Villa had ordered the executions of 300 women in a village near Parral. After taking the village, the sensational news accounts reported, Villa ordered the women of the town herded into the street to see if any federal soldiers had donned dresses to escape the raid. As the women were lined up, one of them drew a gun and fired off a shot at Villa. Unable to tell which woman fired the gun, the rebel leader had them all shot.

Other atrocities were committed. In 1916, the *Villistas* raided the city of Torreón and captured Luis Herrera, an old enemy of Pancho Villa. Like Villa, Herrera had been a leader of *revolucionarios* in Chihuahua, but in 1914 Herrera had supported Carranza, which made him Villa's enemy. Villa ordered Herrera shot, then had his body hung from a telegraph pole at the train station, a peso folded in one hand, and a photograph of Carranza in the other hand.

Villa scored another victory at the town of Rosario in Chihuahua, where he found federal troops had failed to post guards. The *Villistas* swept through town and slaughtered the garrison, killing 1,900 men in battle and taking 600 prisoners. If the prisoners believed they would be shown mercy by Pancho Villa, they were mistaken. Villa had the hapless prisoners lined up and ordered each man shot in the head.

Sometimes, the fighting spilled over onto American territory. Following the Punitive Expedition, American military leaders assigned U.S. Army garrisons to patrol the Mexican border in Arizona, New Mexico and Texas. On June 11, 1919, Villa ordered an assault on Juárez, just across the Rio Grande River from El Paso. The fighting was so fierce that gunfire strayed across the river into El Paso, endangering people and property. An Associated Press reporter described the fighting:

> Many bullets fell in the streets of El Paso yesterday with the resumption of the attack on Juárez by the *Villistas* surrounding the town. One unidentified woman was killed in her home by a bullet fired from the Mexican side. Her residence is four blocks from the Rio Grande.

Villista sharpshooters assault Juárez, the Mexican city located across from El Paso, Texas. The gunfire during the attack was so intense that stray bullets flew across the Rio Grande River and into El Paso, killing innocent civilians. The U.S. Army was forced to chase the *Villistas* into the hills.

The U.S. Army dispatched infantry troops into Juárez to contain the fighting. Four days after the fighting broke out, American cavalry regiments found it necessary to chase the *Villistas* into the hills.

Carranza seemed unable to defeat Pancho Villa in the north. But matters were different with Emiliano Zapata in the south. Since Carranza had assumed the presidency, Zapata had caused him as much trouble as Villa. For years, control of the state of Morelos seesawed back and forth between Carranza and Zapata. Finally, on April 10, 1919, Carranza's agents managed to snare Zapata in a fatal trap. The rebel leader was lured to a meeting with one of Carranza's generals, whom he was led to believe was interested in joining the *Zapatistas*. Instead, the meeting turned out to be an ambush.

For Carranza, the murder of Zapata was a tremendous blunder. Carranza had never enjoyed the overwhelming support of the Mexican people, particularly the lowly peasants who looked on Villa and Zapata as heroes. Zapata was revered by the landless Indians of southern Mexico. Now, a new foe rose up against Carranza in Alvaro Obregón. A rancher from the city of Huatabampo in the state of Sonora, Obregón had joined the revolution late. He had not taken up arms against Porfirio Díaz, but had raised a rebel army to defend Francisco Madero. After Madero's death, Obregón's men fought Victoriano Huerta's troops in Sonora. He soon developed into a master tactician and scored many victories over federal forces. When Carranza assumed power, Obregón supported the First Chief. Obregón's men clashed several times with the *revolucionarios* under Villa and Zapata. In one battle against the *Villistas*, Obregón lost his right arm.

In 1915, Carranza appointed Obregón commander in chief of the Mexican army. For five years, he served under Carranza, but slowly lost faith in the First Chief. In 1917, Carranza's government adopted a constitution which provided for the election of the president, which Carranza won. The constitution specified that the president could serve just one term. Carranza's term was due to expire in 1920.

Yet, Carranza had no desire to give up power. And so his supporters nominated an obscure Mexican politician named Ignacio Bonillas to succeed him. It was clear to everyone that Bonillas would simply be Carranza's puppet, and that the First Chief would continue to wield the true power in Mexico City.

Alvaro Obregón resolved to run for president himself. Carranza regarded Obregón as a threat to his plans, and moved to have Obregón arrested. When word reached Sonora of Carranza's plans, the State Assembly revolted and declared the Sonora governor, Adolfo de la Huerta, the interim president until new elections could he held. The revolutionary fervor in Sonora swept into other Mexican states and gained favor with the country's military leaders. Suddenly, Carranza found himself lacking the support of the army, which in war-torn Mexico was vital to remaining in power. Carranza fled the capital, hoping to make it to Veracruz, where he planned to regroup his followers and mount a comeback. It was not to be. On May 21, 1920, Venustiano Carranza, the First Chief

ALVARO OBREGÓN

Alvaro Obregón served as president of Mexico from 1920 to 1924. Taking office after a decade of civil war, Obregón was a popular leader who was able to instill a large measure of political stability during his administration. He instituted a number of labor and agrarian reforms, securing rights for the peasants that Pancho Villa and other rebel leaders had been unable to achieve through bloodshed.

Perhaps his greatest achievement was overseeing a thaw in the icy relations Mexico had maintained with the United States since Villa's raid on Columbus in 1916.

He left office at the end of his term in 1924, but planned a political comeback in 1928. Obregón never got the chance to run for president again. Like so many other leaders of Mexico during the country's era of revolution, Obregón was assassinated. President Plutarco Elías Calles, who replaced Obregón in 1924, was suspected of ordering the murder, but no proof has ever surfaced that would definitively link Calles with Obregón's death.

Alvaro Obregón, a member of Carranza's army, lost his arm while battling the *Villistas*. Obregón originally supported President Carranza, but eventually turned against him and ran for president himself.

of the Revolution, was murdered while hiding in the village of Tlaxcalantongo.

Pancho Villa began negotiating with the new government. He wanted to lay down his arms and retire to a ranch with the men who chose to join him there. He had envisioned such a place years before, telling John Reed that former soldiers should live together on a *hacienda* where they could raise cattle and grow crops, but remain in training and at military readiness in the event the government would require their services. He said, "My ambition is to live my life in one of those military colonies among my *compañeros* whom I love, who have suffered so long and so deeply with me. I think I would like the government to establish a leather factory there where we could make good saddles and bridles, because I know how to do that; and the rest of the time I would like to work on my little farm, raising cattle and corn. It would be fine, I think, to help make Mexico a happy place."

De la Huerta, the interim president, was not so willing to accommodate Villa's dream. Obregón was also hostile to the rebel leader. Obregón was the true power in Mexico now, and would, in just a few months, win election as president.

De la Huerta dictated to Villa that, while the Mexican government would provide Villa with a grant of land to establish his *hacienda*, only 50 armed men serving as bodyguards would be permitted to live there. Also, Villa would have no hand in the future course of Mexico politics. He would be expected to retire and grow corn.

Villa accepted the terms. On July 27, 1920, Pancho Villa surrendered to General Eugenio Martínez in Torreón.

"Much rejoicing throughout Mexico is reported, with celebrations being arranged," reported The Associated Press. "Villa was restored to full citizenship . . . He also was given a yearly allowance by the Mexican government . . . and his men were restored to citizenship and given farming lands."

Torreón, Mexico, as it appeared in 1920, when Villa finally surrendered to Mexican authorities. Just seven years earlier, in 1913, this important rail junction was the target of a *Villista* raid in which Villa's enemy Luis Herrera, a supporter of Carranza, was shot and hung in the town's train station.

Villa settled on a *hacienda* known as Canutillo in the state of Durango. It was a tremendous prize for a man so hated by the government, comprising some 163,000 acres, including 4,400 acres of rich irrigated farmland. Before the revolution, it had been owned by a wealthy *hacendado*; over the years, though, Canutillo suffered from neglect and was in need of many repairs. Villa set about converting it into a working ranch that would provide a home for his men and many Mexicans who wished to find work there.

Villa had the buildings, stables and warehouses repaired. A post office, telegraph station and flourmill were erected. The former rebel chief was most proud of the school he constructed on the *hacienda*'s grounds. "It's going to be the best school I know how to start and every child on this ranch is going to attend," Villa told an American newspaper reporter in 1921. "Schools are what Mexico needs above everything else. If I was at the head of things I would put plenty of schools in the cities and towns and besides, I'd put a school on every *hacienda* and ranch."

Villa was joined at Canutillo by some of the children he had fathered over the years. As a *revolucionario* constantly on the run, Villa rarely had the opportunity to enjoy the company of his many sons and daughters. But now at Canutillo, three sons and four daughters moved in with their father. By now he had taken a new wife, and she bore him two more sons at Canutillo.

Life at Canutillo seemed idyllic for Pancho Villa, but he was deeply troubled. Since retiring, the rebel leader found himself mistrustful of Obregón and the officials who served under him. And so Villa took steps to protect himself. Villa had sniper posts built into the *hacienda*'s walls — places where armed men could station themselves and defend Canutillo from an assault. What's more, the men who lived on the *hacienda* were expected to drill and maintain a military readiness. Ralph Parker, an American mining engineer who visited Canutillo in 1920, reported that it was nothing less than an armed camp. "Bugles sounded at 6 A.M., an hour before daylight, and again in the evening, and at intervals during the day," Parker reported.

"Everyone including myself followed orders for meals, lights out, et cetera."

Parker also said that Villa regularly ordered the men lined up for inspection, and that the former rebel leader insisted on being addressed as "general." This attention to military preparedness may have distressed officials of the Obregón government in Mexico City. After all, Villa was supposed to retire quietly to Canutillo to raise corn—not drill his troops. What's more, the election of 1924 was soon on the horizon. Under the constitution in place, Alvaro Obregón could not run for re-election and, unlike his predecessors, he had no desire to defy the law by ignoring the constitution or by running a puppet candidate in his place. A poll conducted in 1922 by the newspaper *El Universal* showed that the four men with the most popular support for the presidency in 1922 were Carlos B. Zetinia, a member of the Mexican Senate; De la Huerta, the former interim president; Plutarco Elías Calles, a strong-willed political leader from Sonora, and—to the surprise of many of Mexico's political leaders— Pancho Villa.

Their surprise soon turned to alarm when Villa granted an interview to Regino Hernández Llergo, a reporter for *El Universal.* During the interview, Villa told Llergo that he was considering running for governor of Durango. Villa said:

> The affair of my candidacy for the governorship of Durango is of little importance for me right now, but it will show you the enormous support I have . . . I am enormously popular sir. . . my race loves me. I have friends in all social groups, among the rich, the poor, the educated, and the ignorant . . . Sir, I do not believe that anyone has the support that Francisco Villa has . . . For this reason the politicians are afraid of me. They are afraid of me because they know on the day that I decide to fight, I shall destroy them.

For the leaders of the Mexican government who wished only to put the long years of their country's civil war behind them, those words carried a chilling and ominous tone they did not wish to hear repeated.

On July 19, 1923, Pancho Villa traveled to the village of Rio Florido to attend the baptism of a friend's child. Villa was to be honored at the baptism by being named godfather to the boy, a role he had assumed many times before. Instead of riding to Rio Florido on horseback, Villa went in a large Dodge touring car that he recently had acquired. Five bodyguards accompanied him that morning. Villa carried two Colt 45 pistols strapped to his hips.

Historians still have not identified who sent the assassins that were stationed along the road to Rio Florido as Villa drove through the city of Parral. Waiting in an apartment building, they nearly shot Villa when his car stopped at the intersection of Juárez and Barreda streets. He was saved when school children stepped into the street in front of the car. Unaware of how close he came to death that morning, Villa motored on and reached Rio Florido, where he participated in the baptismal ceremony.

He planned to return to Canutillo the next morning. Again, his route home took him through Parral. This time, when the Dodge stopped at the intersection of Juárez and Barreda streets, a man stepped out into the street and shouted the old war cry of the Division del Norte.

"*Viva Villa!*" he shouted.

At this alert, the assassins stationed in the apartment building opened fire. Villa slammed his foot onto the accelerator and roared toward the snipers. Bullets riddled the car and the Dodge struck a tree and rolled over. Villa's body was thrown from the car. The snipers kept firing at the body of the *revolucionario* sprawled across the dusty street. Medical examiners would later find 47 bullet holes in the body of Pancho Villa.

Pancho Villa spent his later years residing on a ranch with his family. Though Villa was to retire from political life, he ran his residence as though it were an army camp, eliciting distrust among government leaders.

Two of Villa's bodyguards were killed in the melee; three others were wounded but escaped.

The next day, Pancho Villa was buried in a cemetery in Parral. A simple stone slab marked his grave.

Chronology

1810   Miguel Hidalgo leads the first Mexican uprising against Spain.

1821   Mexico is granted independence.

1877   Porfirio Díaz assumes presidency.

1878   Doroteo Arango is born June 5 in Durango; later changes name to Francisco Villa.

1894   Villa shoots his sister's rapist, then flees into the mountains and becomes a bandit.

1908   Díaz tells an American journalist he will permit free elections; Francisco Madero resolves to run for president.

1910   Díaz has Madero arrested and forced into exile; Villa raises an army and defeats federal troops at a train station in San Andrés.

1911   Villa's siege of Juárez forces Díaz to resign; Madero elected president.

1912   Villa imprisoned in Santiago Tlatelolco; escapes on Christmas Day and flees to Texas.

1913   General Victoriano Huerta seizes presidency in an American-backed coup; Madero assassinated on Huerta's orders. Villa returns to Mexico and raises an army.

1914   American writer John Reed rides with Villa and reports on the revolution; in February, Villa kills Englishman William S. Benton, touching off an international incident; in April, American Marines invade the port city of Veracruz; in July, Huerta resigns and Venustiano Carranza becomes president.

1915   With assistance from America, federal troops defeat Villa's men at Agua Prieta.

1916 In January, *Villistas* massacre 18 American mining engineers near Santa Isabel; in March, Villa attacks Columbus, New Mexico, killing 17 Americans. General John J. Pershing leads the Punitive Expedition into Mexico.

1917 Pershing returns to the United States after failing to find Villa.

1919 Rebel leader Emiliano Zapata assassinated on Carranza's orders.

1920 Alvaro Obregón elected president; Carranza assassinated. Villa surrenders and retires to a Durango ranch.

1923 Villa is assassinated in Parral.

Bibliography

Katz, Friedrich. *The Life and Times of Pancho Villa.* Stanford, California: Stanford University Press, 1998.

Lansford, William Douglas. *Pancho Villa.* Los Angeles: Sherbourne Press, 1965.

Lopez, Enrique Hank. "Mexico." *American Heritage,* April 1969.

Lopez, Enrique Hank. "Papa and Pancho Villa." *American Heritage,* August 1970.

Mason, Herbert Molloy Jr. *The Great Pursuit: Pershing's Expedition to Destroy Pancho Villa.* New York: Smithmark Publishers, 1970.

O'Malley, Ilene V. *The Myth of the Revolution.* New York: Greenwood Press, 1986.

Palmer, Frederick. *John J. Pershing: General of the Armies.* Harrisburg, Pennsylvania: Military Service Publishing Company, 1948.

Pinchon, Edgcumb. *Viva Villa!* New York: Harcourt, Brace and Company, 1933.

Reed, John. *Insurgent Mexico.* New York: Clarion Books, 1969.

Wolfe, Bertram D. "The Harvard Man in the Kremlin Wall." *American Heritage,* February 1960.

Wolff, Leon. "Black Jack's Mexican Goose Chase." *American Heritage,* June 1962.

"Battle Begins at Juárez Gate." *The San Francisco Call,* June 12, 1919.

"Carranza May Fight." *The San Francisco Bulletin,* March 11, 1916.

"General Pershing Pursues Bandits." *The San Francisco Bulletin,* March 16, 1916.

"Latin America." *Time,* July 30, 1923.

"U.S. Cavalry Chasing Villistas." *Honolulu Star-Bulletin,* June 16, 1919.

"U.S. Ready for Dash, Cavalry to Lead Advance." *The San Francisco Bulletin*, March 14, 1916.

"Villa Gives Up; Cantu Revolts!" *The San Francisco Bulletin*, July 28, 1920.

"Villa Slays 300 Women in Revenge." *The San Francisco Call*, June 18, 1920.

Websites

Biography of James Creelman
http://www.limavady.com/jamesc.html

Pancho Villa State Park
*http://www.emnrd.state.nm.us/nmparks/PAGES/PARKS/
PANCHO/PANCHO.HTM*

Mexican Revolution
http://www.skalman.nu/history/mexican-rev.htm

Pancho Villa Home Page
http://ojinaga.com/villa

The Biography Project: Pancho Villa
http://www.popsubculture.com/pop/bio-project/pancho-villa.html

Further Reading

Clendenen, Clarence. *Blood on the Border: The United States Army and the Mexican Irregulars.* New York: Macmilan, 1969.

Dulles, John W. F. *Yesterday in Mexico: A Chronicle of the Revolution.* Austin, Texas: University of Texas Press, 1961.

Gilly, Adolfo. *The Mexican Revolution.* Norfolk, England: Thetford Press Ltd., 1983.

Guzman, Martin Luis. *Memoirs of Pancho Villa.* Austin, Texas: University of Texas Press, 1975.

Hall, Linda. *Revolution on the Border: The United States and Mexico, 1910-1920.* Albuquerque, New Mexico: University of New Mexico Press, 1988.

Katz, Friedrich. *The Life and Times of Pancho Villa.* Stanford, California: Stanford University Press, 1998.

Lansford, William Douglas. *Pancho Villa.* Los Angeles: Sherbourne Press, 1965.

Martinez, Oscar J. *Fragments of the Mexican Revolution: Personal Accounts from the Border.* Albuquerque, New Mexico: University of New Mexico Press, 1983.

Mason, Herbert Molloy Jr. *The Great Pursuit: Pershing's Expedition to Destroy Pancho Villa.* New York: Smithmark Publishers, 1970.

Meyer, Michael C. and William L. Sherman. *The Course of Mexican History.* New York: Oxford University Press, 1979.

O'Malley, Ilene V. *The Myth of the Revolution.* New York: Greenwood Press, 1986.

Palmer, Frederick. *John J. Pershing: General of the Armies.* Harrisburg, Pennsylvania: Military Service Publishing Company, 1948.

Pinchon, Edgcumb. *Viva Villa!* New York: Harcourt, Brace and Company, 1933.

Quirk, Robert E. *An Affair of Honor: Woodrow Wilson and the Occupation of Veracruz.* New York: W.W. Norton, 1962.

Reed, John. *Insurgent Mexico.* New York: Clarion Books, 1969.

Stein, R. Conrad. *The Mexican Revolution 1910-1920.* New York: New Discovery Books, 1994.

Turner, John K. *Barbarous Mexico.* Austin, Texas: University of Texas Press, 1969.

Vanderwood, Paul J., and Frank N. Samponaro. *Border Fury: A Picture Postcard of Mexico's Revolution and U.S. War Preparedness, 1910-1917.* Albuquerque, New Mexico: University of New Mexico Press, 1988.

Wilkie, James W. and Albert L. Michaels, eds. *Revolution in Mexico: Years of Upheaval, 1910-1940.* New York: Alfred A. Knopf, 1969.

Womack, John. *Zapata and the Mexican Revolution.* New York: Alfred A. Knopf, 1970.

Index

Picture Credits

About the Author

Hal Marcovitz is a journalist for *The Morning Call*, a newspaper based in Allentown, Pennsylvania. He has written more than 40 books for young readers. His other title in the THE GREAT HISPANIC HERITAGE series is a biography of farm labor leader Cesar Chavez. He makes his home in Chalfont, Pennsylvania, with his wife, Gail, and daughters Michelle and Ashley.